THE MIDDLE EAS

Lawrence and Wishart Limited
39 Museum Street
London WC1A 1LQ

First published in French as *Proche Orient Une Guerre de Cent Ans*
by Editions Sociales, Paris 1984

This English edition first published 1988
© Lawrence and Wishart Ltd, 1988

Photoset in North Wales by
Derek Doyle & Associates, Mold, Clwyd
Printed and bound in Great Britain by
The Camelot Press Ltd, Southampton

The Middle East:
War Without End?

Alain Gresh and Dominique Vidal

translated by Simon Medaney with Henriette Bardel

LAWRENCE AND WISHART
LONDON

Contents

Introduction

'The Promised Land' is sacred to three religions. But up until now the promised land has not lived up to its name – it has been the scene of trauma, grief and exile.

In 1882 the first rising (*Aliyah*) began, signalling the start of a massive 'return' of Jews to Zion. In 1982 the Israeli army seized control of an Arab capital for the first time. Between these dates a war went on for a hundred years – and it is still raging.

At the very heart of this tragedy lies a people which has been gradually dispossessed and scattered. A quarter of them live in occupied territory. The other three-quarters exist from one exodus to another and from one massacre to the next.

Five major conflicts since the Second World War have been fought over the issue of their country: in 1947-49, 1956, 1967, 1973 and most recently in 1982. On the Israeli side 10,000 men have died in these conflicts alone while on the Arab side at least ten times as many have perished. And perhaps someone, somewhere is contemplating another outbreak in order to settle things once and for all.

The region has been ravaged by other evils which are to a certain extent connected to the Israeli-Palestinian conflict. In spite of short periods of respite, ruthless civil war continues to rage in Lebanon. The Kurds have been scattered like the Palestinians, and persecuted in Turkey, Iran and Iraq. The Islamic Revolution appears to have exhausted itself and has degenerated into a confrontation with Baghdad which has already cost half a million lives.

War, war and war again. Why? Public opinion can't make head or tail of it. The Middle East seems an insoluble mystery. Day after day television, radio and the press

churn out large amounts of news which is one-sided,
biased and indeed tendentious: everyone knows that the
Israeli leadership has committed supporters in the media,
whose support for Israel sometimes expresses itself in
their journalism. It certainly seems that events defy
understanding. Two recent examples are particularly
revealing: Syria, enemy of Israel and the USA, her army
fighting Israel in Lebanon, tried to wipe out the P.L.O.;
and Yasser Arafat, just after getting out of a trap in
Tripoli – thanks to the French bombardment of Baalbec –
went off to see President Mubarak whose country had
signed the Camp David agreement with Israel. The
'surprise' and 'confusion' expressed by some people when
these events became known is indicative of how little is
understood about what is really going on in the region.

We have had to come to terms with these problems
ourselves. We have covered Middle Eastern affairs for
several years now, mainly for the French weekly
Revolution. It was this experience which prompted us to set
to work on this book. Every article we wrote made us
realise the need to get at the roots of current events in a
way which was just not possible within the confines of a
weekly magazine. Firstly the historical context: the causes
of the present day conflict go back to the partition of the
Ottoman Empire, and then, via rivalry between imperial
powers, to the partition of Palestine. In the Middle East
more than anywhere else the weight of the past lies heavily
on the present. Next we have to take account of the
economic, social, political, ideological and cultural
characteristics of the countries and their peoples: the
so-called geopolitical view all too often excludes analysis of
these fundamental elements. Our third task is to
distinguish as carefully as possible between the purely
national, or regional, aspects of what is happening and
those that relate to the involvement of outside powers.
Only by coming to terms with these diverse factors can we
shed light on the way the Middle East works. This is a far
larger task than can be accomplished within the confines
of this little book. Our aim has simply been to make a small
but significant contribution to it.

These objectives have determined the structure of the book. In the first chapter we have dealt very rapidly with the main events in Middle Eastern history from the Ottoman Empire to the invasion of Lebanon. The second chapter focuses on Israel, looking at Zionism, the inter-war creation of the 'nation' of Israel within the *Yishuv* movement, the setting up of the State and the contradictions inherent in it. The third chapter is devoted to the study of the Palestinians, their history, their economic, social and political characteristics, and the evolution of the P.L.O. The fourth chapter deals with Lebanon, the political and religious divisions leading to civil war and the foreign influences bearing on it. The fifth and last chapter looks at the part played by both the world powers – the U.S.S.R., the United States and France – and by other countries in the area – Egypt, Syria, Saudi Arabia, Iraq and Jordan. In our conclusion we examine the different proposals which have been put forward to resolve the Palestinian problem; these remain the only key to a peaceful future.

The Arab-Israeli conflict has given rise to a considerable amount of literature, much of which is excellent. Despite all the specialised studies we felt that there was a book missing: one that would be accessible without being oversimplified; one that would take an overall view whilst taking all aspects of the situation into consideration; politically committed of course – who isn't? – but not biased or simply a vehicle for propaganda; that would be up to date but with its roots firmly in the historical background to present events. These are the main features of what we have tried to do. We do not have a clear idea of who our readers will be. We have tried to write for the informed reader as well as for readers new to the Middle Eastern question, for the reader who sympathises with the Palestinians as well as for supporters of Israel who want to be better informed.

We would like to take this opportunity to thank Joseph Algazy, Rina Cohen, Elisabeth Picard, Christine Queralt, Jacques Sephila and Eric Venturini. Without their careful and critical reading of the drafts the book would not be what it is today.

Chapter 1

The Roots of the Problem

The conflicts between Israel and the Palestinians and Arabs are not new. Their roots go far back into the distant past of the Middle East, and to biblical times – to which we will refer in the second chapter. A basic knowledge of the history of the past few decades is essential for an understanding of the present. To try to sum up such a complex history in a few pages might seem an impossible task; however a condensed overview of the region's troubled past will shed light on its equally troubled present. Thus a necessarily brief, and occasionally schematic, approach to the history of Zionism and Israel, the Palestinian movement and Lebanon cannot be avoided.

The Sick Man of Europe

'The sick man of Europe' was how Nicholas I, Tsar of All the Russians, described the Ottoman Empire. From the end of the eighteenth century this 'sickness' obsessed all the chancellories of Europe; the 'Eastern Question', or the problem of sharing out the huge possessions of the Ottoman Empire, had a determining influence on the whole of nineteenth century history.

Starting in Asia Minor, from where they had begun their expansion in the thirteenth century, the Ottoman Turks aimed at the conquest of the whole world. By the fourteenth century they had settled in Greece, Serbia and Bulgaria. Constantinople, capital of the Byzantine Empire, fell in 1453. The Balkans, Asia Minor and the Black Sea,

11

which now became a Turkish 'lake', were conquered in the next twenty years. In the wake of Mohammed the Conqueror, Selim I (1512-1520) seized control of the Arab world: Mesopotamia, Egypt, Syria and a part of the Arabian Peninsula. His successor, Suleiman the Magnificent, annexed Belgrade and most of Hungary and Transylvania. He reached Baghdad in the east, the Arabian coast in the south and North Africa in the west. When he died, in 1556, the Ottoman yoke extended from the gates of Vienna to Aden, from the Caspian Sea to Algiers. The Turks controlled three seas: the Mediterranean, the Black Sea and the Red Sea, as well as part of the Indian Ocean. They controlled the major lines of communication. They ruled over a score of nations comprising over fifty million people. At the time the population of France was sixteen million and England five million. It was the summit and also the beginning of the decline of Turkish power.

In explaining the weakening and subsequent disintegration of an empire a number of interconnecting factors need to be borne in mind. The heavily centralised Ottoman edifice suffered initially from internal crisis: incompetent sultans, corrupt administration, an elite janissary corps which had become like an hereditary caste and the exhaustion of financial resources coming from conquest. The great European powers – Britain, France and Russia – first put a stop to Ottoman expansion and then occupied parts of the Empire themselves. At the same time, from within the Empire itself, from the Balkans to the Arab world, came pressure from growing nationalist movements, not to mention the Kurds and the Armenians.

By the end of the nineteenth century the dismembering was well on its way. The autonomy of Bulgaria, the independence of Serbia, Romania and Montenegro, and the Austrian occupation of Bosnia and Herzegovina had been ratified by the Treaty of Berlin in 1878. By the end of the 1912-1913 war the Empire had lost all of its possessions in Europe except Thrace. In North Africa the French had occupied Algeria in 1830, and then Tunisia and Morocco, while the Italians had landed in Libya in 1912. The Middle Eastern part of the Empire had also been torn apart: the British had seized Aden in 1839, then Egypt, in 1882, and the Sudan. They also assumed 'protection' over the whole of the Persian Gulf. In the Arabian Peninsula the Najd was in Wahhabi hands and the Hejaz under Hashemite control. Mount Lebanon had become autonomous, under French 'protection'.

'How can we fail to blame ourselves as we stand by and watch while foreigners unjustly seize our countries, humiliate our people and shed the innocent blood of our brothers?' exclaimed the Syrian Rashid Rida in 1883. European intervention in the Arab world awakened both Islamic reformism and Arab nationalism. After the adventure of Mohammed Ali who, with French help, set up an independent Syro-Egyptian state between 1831 and 1840, came the Nahda, a cultural and linguistic renaissance, Al Afghani 'The Renovator', and the growth of a variety of sects and parties. The Decentralisation Party was founded in Cairo in 1912. The following year saw the first Arab Congress in Paris. The constitutional movement was founded in Morocco and a nationalist party was set up in Tunisia. As a result Western capitals, and London in particular, were confronted with an obstacle which could only increase in size.

At Daggers Drawn

Western countries sought in the Ottoman Empire the same things that they sought throughout their colonial possessions: access to cheap raw materials – particularly oil from the beginning of the twentieth century – profitable investment opportunities, vast markets for their domestic production and control of the main lines of communication.

Naturally with each power acting in its own interests conflicts were bound to occur. Until the end of the nineteenth century there was a consensus of interests uniting Great Britain, France and Germany, with the addition of Russia from 1878 onwards when the Tsars' own expansionist pretensions were halted. This consensus was based on the need to bolster the Ottoman Empire. But once this consensus came to an end a series of conflicts

began. Once Constantinople had allied itself to the central
European powers – Germany and Austro-Hungary – and
had thereby been associated with them in their defeat in
the First World War, partition became inevitable. From
the beginning of the twentieth century all of the colonial
powers prepared to stake their claims.

France could claim seniority: in 1535 Francois I had
been the first European ruler to extract 'capitulations', or
privileges, from the Sultan for France and French
nationals within the Ottoman Empire. Since 1639 France
had 'protected' the Maronite Christians in Lebanon and
had mounted several military operations in their 'defence'.
Its role as 'protector' of the catholic Holy Places in
Palestine had also been recognised. The French dominated North Africa, and in Egypt retained the influence
they had established at the time of Napoleon's campaign,
which had led to the construction of the Suez Canal. While
they had had to give up dreams of establishing a protected
'*pashalik*' from Morocco to Sinai, as well as the idea of a
Syro-Egyptian state, they still held on to powerful
positions in the commercial and banking fields: France
was Constantinople's foremost creditor. Last but not least
it had considerable cultural influence, largely due to a
network of more than 500 schools. At the outbreak of the
First World War France's aims were to preserve its
commercial ties and to retain control over its spheres of
interest. The expansion of British power was in full flow.
The Middle East was the life line between Britain and
India – the jewel in the crown of the empire. The security
of both land and sea routes between London and Delhi
depended on British control of the region. The speed of
growth of British power was staggering: control of Malta
in 1815; protection of the Barbary Coast and the Emirates
in the Persian Gulf in 1820; seizure of Aden and Oman in
1839 followed by Cyprus in 1878; purchase of the Suez
Canal Company in 1875; and control of Egypt in 1882,
after crushing the revolt led by Arabi Pasha. This was
followed in 1898 by the acquisition of Sudan. Between
1886 and 1914 they acquired protectorates on the
southern coast of the Arabian peninsula. British interests
spread throughout these countries and even as far as

Persia which was split into zones of influence by an agreement with Tsarist Russia in 1907, in the name of the Anglo-Persian Oil Company, later to be taken over by the Admiralty. Clearly, British policy was to maintain secure positions and then to expand, chiefly in the directions of Iraq and Palestine, so as to replace the unreliable Ottoman Empire by a defensive line protecting the main channels of communication to India.

Russia had only one aim regarding the Ottoman Empire: to control the Black Sea and the Bosphorus and thereby access to the Mediterranean and the trade routes. On the eve of the First World War 40% of Russian exports and 54% of its maritime traffic passed through the straits. This search for 'warm waters' explains the innumerable Russo-Turkish conflicts throughout many centuries. The Treaty of Berlin in 1878 having frustrated the Russians' hoped for victory over the Ottoman Empire, they now allied themselves with France and Great Britain in the hope of ensuring safe access to the Mediterranean. They also planned to extend their influence in Persia.

In contrast to its rivals Germany had no colonial possessions in the Ottoman Empire, but had greatly increased her economic, political and military involvement in Turkey by the end of the nineteenth century. Following Kaiser Wilhelm II's visits to the sultan, Germany had obtained the valuable contract to build the Constantinople-Baghdad railway. German investments increased considerably: from virtually nothing in 1880, they rose to 34 million marks by 1900 and to 110 million in 1910. In 1881 General Von Der Goltz had been given the task of reorganising the Turkish army. In 1913 it was commanded by another German General – Liman Von Sanders.

Both Italy and Greece had claims too. Italy became involved in the war to 'legitimise' her control over Eritrea, Libya and the Dodecanese Islands in the Aegean. Greece claimed Smyrna and the surrounding region on the grounds of historical ties between the two sides of the sea.

These claims, or at least those of the future victors in the First World War, were staked in the form of treaties and secret agreements. Thus in 1915 there was the Constanti-

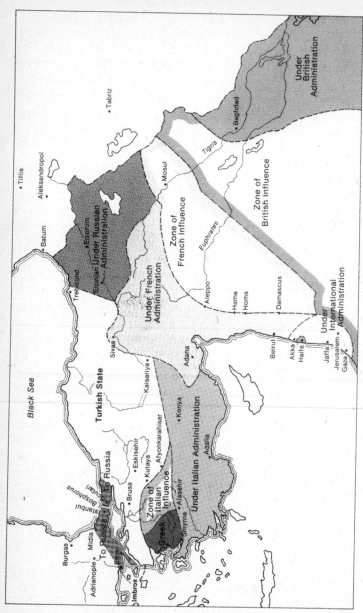

The partitioning of Turkey according to the secret agreements of 1915–1917

nople Agreement between Russia, Britain and France: in April of the same year Italy joined them in signing the Treaty of London; in 1916 came the Sykes-Picot-Sazonov Agreement between London, Paris and Moscow; and finally there was the St Jean de Maurienne agreement between Italy, France and Britain. It was not until the Bolshevik revolution brought this secret diplomacy to an end that the people of these countries discovered what the Great Powers had secretly agreed on their behalf. When it came to light it had considerable repercussions, and served to add fuel to anti-imperialist feelings in the Middle East.

The end result of these deals was that the Ottoman Empire was carved up in a quite arbitrary manner: national and popular aspirations were ignored in favour of colonial interests. The map opposite shows how Tsarist Russia took over the north-eastern part of the Empire, Constantinople, the western side of the Bosphorus, the Sea of Marmara, the Dardanelles and part of the Black Sea coast of Asia Minor. However, both the harbour of Constantinople and the straits remained open to the Allied fleets. Anatolia was chopped up: in the middle a small Turkish state, to the south an area under Italian control or influence, and part of the west coast annexed by Greece. France acquired Cilicia and the Vilayet of Adana. The Arab Middle East was divided between France and Britain. France controlled the coastline of Syria and Lebanon, and an area roughly corresponding to present-day Syria, as well as the oil-producing area of Mosul, which Clemenceau ceded to Britain after his meeting with Lloyd George in December 1918. Great Britain acquired control of Eastern Mesopotamia, and recognition of its influence in the West and the area that is now Jordan. The two 'areas of influence' were intended to form a state or a confederation of Arab states. Palestine meanwhile became an international zone, apart from the ports of Haifa and Acre which came under British rule.

These agreements were only carried out in part: a case of counting the chickens before they were hatched. The Soviet leaders repudiated the Tsarist demands. Between 1919 and 1922 the Turkish nationalists, led by Mustapha

Kemal, liberated Anatolia from the French, Italian and Greek occupiers who had been there since the Armistice. For Britain, who had promised everything to everyone, the moment of truth had arrived.

Perfidious Albion

'Better to win and perjure yourself than to lose.' So said Lawrence of Arabia, the British colonel who was the architect of the 'Arab Revolt'. Great Britain had indeed won the war, but to do so it had perjured itself many times over. In order to be sure of a wide range of alliances Britain had 'sold' the Middle East three times over.

Firstly, as we have just seen, to the French, whose control of Syria and Lebanon was recognised by the Sykes-Picot Agreement.

Secondly to the Arabs. It was vital to reach agreement with the Arabs for two reasons: to counter the Jihad (Holy War) decreed by the Sultan of Constantinople in his capacity of 'Leader of the Faithful'; and to prevent any possible alliance between Germany, Turkey and the Arabs. Two sets of negotiations began: with the Wahhabi leader Ibn Saud, ruler of the Najd, and the Hashemite Hussein, ruler of the Hejaz. Between the two they governed by far the greater part of the Arabian peninsula. In December 1915 Sir Percy Cox, the British Resident in the Gulf, and Ibn Saud, signed the first Anglo-Arab agreement. The second agreement, which was more significant, was finally concluded after lengthy exchanges of letters between Sir Henry MacMahon, British High Commissioner in Cairo, and Sharif Hussein, protector of the holy cities of Mecca and Medina, and a descendant of the Prophet. London agreed to 'recognise and support Arab independence', while Hussein set to work to foment the 'Arab Revolt'. From June 1916 thousands of his soldiers supported contingents of British troops on the Middle Eastern front – often with decisive results. Hussein, who was worried about the Sykes-Picot Agreement and the Balfour Declaration, was outmanoeuvred by London in February 1918. A declaration reaffirming the undertakings made by the British government concerning the liberation of the Arab peoples was communicated to him. The small print of the text shows that only the coastal region of Syria – 'bounded in the east by the districts of Damascus, Homs, Hama and Aleppo' – more or less present-day Lebanon – was excluded from the future Arab State.

Lastly to the Zionists. The British needed to have the Zionist movement on their side for several reasons. They hoped to bring the United States – where there was already a powerful Jewish lobby – into the war. By so doing the British government hoped to induce the German and Austro-Hungarian Jews to withdraw support from their governments. They even thought in terms of limiting the impact of the Russian Revolution, many of whose leaders, particularly among the Bolsheviks, were Jews: it was hoped to counteract the effect of Russian withdrawal from the Eastern Front. The more farsighted elements believed the prophecy of the founder of Zionism, Theodore Herzl, claiming that the Jewish state would constitute 'an outpost of civilisation against barbarianism'. Put in simple terms, a Jewish national homeland would prevent the establishment of any foreign influence in Palestine. Sir Herbert Samuel told the cabinet in 1915 that 'The establishment of a great European power – France – so close to the Suez Canal would represent a permanent, and major, threat to the Empire's vital lines of communication'. After long negotiation between the British government, Zionist leaders, and representatives of British anti-Zionist Jews his majesty's government ratified the now famous letter written by the foreign secretary, Lord Balfour, to Lord Rothschild, dated 2 November 1917. In Arthur Koestler's words, 'One nation solemnly undertook to give another nation's territory to a third'. Balfour stated that Great Britain would 'view with favour the establishment in Palestine of a national home for the Jewish people, and will use their best endeavours to facilitate the achievement of this object'.

It was hardly surprising, then, that a peace treaty covering the Middle East proved extremely difficult to draw up. It took eighteen months of intensive negotiations before the 1920 San Remo conference sorted out the mess

created by British undertakings. Arab demands for the
implementation of the agreement promising them self
determination were rejected, by both the French, who
would have lost Syria and Lebanon, and by the Zionists. In
1920 there were less than 70,000 Jews and more than
800,000 Arabs in Palestine: freedom of choice would
inevitably have led to the setting up of an Arab state. The
United States, where President Wilson's high-sounding
principles were in reality no more than a cover for a desire
to take over from Britain and France in the area,
reluctantly accepted the proposal, but only provisionally.
Since the great colonial powers' diplomats lacked any
imagination, they dreamed up the idea of the 'mandate.'
According to the French High Commissioner it was 'a
provisional arrangement designed to enable a population
that is, politically speaking, immature to educate itself in
such a way as to prepare for self-government one day'.
The 'principles' then were apparently safeguarded and
the great powers could grab what they wanted – France
acquired the Syrian 'mandate' and Britain the Iraqi and
Palestinian 'mandates'. The Palestinian mandate, minus
Transjordan, and including the Balfour Declaration, was
ratified by the League of Nations on 24 July 1922. Oil was
not overlooked in the peace agreement: France and
Britain were to share the exploitation of the Mosul oil
fields, Britain retaining its 75% stake and France taking
over Germany's 25%. A pipeline would be built to link
Mosul to the Mediterranean via the French Mandate.
What Lenin called this 'imperialist robbery' was ratified by
the Treaty of Sevres, signed by the allies and the Ottoman
government on 10 August 1920.

Birth of New States

Nobody was taken in by the hypocrisy of the mandates,
and certainly not the Arabs, whose aspirations to
independence were stronger than ever at the end of the
war. Originally aimed against the Ottoman empire and its
allies, the Arab revolt soon turned against the new colonial
powers: Britain, which had initially provoked it, and
France. Although the new frontiers drawn up by the great

powers were gradually imposed despite Arab desires for a unified state, they served only to delineate the area in which the struggle was to take place. While the nationalist forces were not yet strong enough to throw off the imperialist stranglehold on the region, their strength steadily increased in almost all the countries in the area, although the form they took and pace at which they developed varied from area to area. A short, and therefore schematic, survey of what occurred is particularly necessary because the events which began then were to shape the Middle East as it is today.

In October 1918 Feisal, one of Sharif Hussein's sons, entered Damascus with his own forces, and with British troops. A Franco-British declaration dated 7th November of that year foresaw the possibility of independence for both Syria and Iraq at some stage in the future. This corresponded to the demands of the Syrian, Lebanese and Palestinian nationalists formulated at the General Congress of Syria in July 1919: rejection of the Sykes-Picot Agreement and the Balfour Declaration, and support for independence without partition or protection. A new congress in March 1920 proclaimed the independence of Greater Syria, opted for a constitutional monarchy and 'elected' Feisal as king. But what the members of the congress did not know was that Feisal had already accepted the principle of partition: he had promised Lebanon to France and had 'made arrangements' for Palestine. In 1919 he had written to the Zionist leader Felix Frankfurter 'We are working together to bring about the rebirth of a reformed and revitalised Middle East, in which our two movements shall complement each other. The Jewish movement is nationalist, not imperialist ... There is room for both of us in Syria'.

But the French wanted the lot: using their Syrian 'mandate' they presented an ultimatum to Feisal on 14 July; ten days later, after a fierce struggle, General Gouraud arrived in Damascus at the head of his troops, where he dethroned and expelled the king. After the Treaty of Sevres in September 1920 Syria – already minus Palestine and Transjordan – was carved up despite popular resistance. Four states were created: Greater

Lebanon (which included Tripoli, the Bekaa Valley, Tyre
and Sidon), Damascus, Aleppo and an Alawi state. In 1922
the last three formed a federation while the Druze Jebel
became autonomous. The Sanjak of Alexandretta was set
up in 1924, and was ultimately ceded by France to Turkey
in 1939. In a redistribution in 1925 the states of Aleppo
and Damascus merged to form Syria. All this messing
about only served to irritate the population of countries
whose frontiers were continually subject to change without
any consultation whatsoever: as a result there was an
uprising in the Druze Jebel in July 1925 which quickly
spread throughout the country. In an effort to suppress it
the French army went so far as to shell Damascus.

It was at this point that the history of Syria and Lebanon
separated. In 1926 Lebanon became a parliamentary
republic linked to France, although it was not until 1936
that the Popular Front government offered her independence in exchange for an alliance involving military bases
and facilities for the French armed forces. A similar treaty
was signed between France and Syria in 1936 after the
French High Commissioner in Damascus had dissolved
the first Constituent Assembly in 1928, thinking it to be
too nationalist, and had proclaimed a new constitution in
1930 incorporating an electoral system which ensured the
election of a more 'moderate' assembly in 1932. Neither of
these treaties was ever ratified owing to the early demise of
the Popular Front in France. It was not until 1941 that
General Catroux, acting as General de Gaulle's representative, proclaimed the independence of Syria and
Lebanon.

The nationalist movement was equally powerful in Iraq.
There had been a popular insurrection against the Turks
in 1915-1916, bolstered by many Iraqi officers who had
taken part in the 'Arab revolt'. At the same time as the
Congress of Syria was going on in Damascus in March
1920 a National Congress of Iraq was also taking place,
proclaiming independence and offering the crown to
Abdullah, brother of Feisal. When the British mandate
was announced in April it served only to add fuel to the
flames: it took 150,000 British troops six months and a
great deal of difficulty to put down the insurrection which

ensued. The British then put Feisal on the throne of Iraq: the same Feisal who had been thrown out of Syria. His coronation, on the 23 August 1923 was 'legitimised' by a plebiscite. Nationalist rumblings continued unabated and forced the British to sign a treaty in October 1922 which brought the mandate to an end. Henceforth British economic, military and strategic hegemony in Iraq was at the request of the Iraqi government. In the wake of continuing popular unrest two more treaties followed before the treaty of 1930 which finally granted complete independence to Iraq in exchange for military bases and facilities and consultation with Britain on matters relating to defence and foreign affairs. Iraq then entered the League of Nations on 3 October 1932. The nationalist movement culminated in October 1936 with a putsch led by officers allied to a front composed of the nationalist Ahali movement, trade unionists and communists. However, General Bekr Sidki and his co-conspirators, worried by the Front's progressive plans, did an about-turn. Before his assassination in August 1937 Bekr Sidki had time to sign the first – and, as we shall see, by no means the last – Baghdad Pact, grouping Iraq with Iran, Turkey and Afghanistan.

The nationalist movement in Palestine was even more militant than its allies in Damascus and Baghdad, because it had to confront two opponents: Britain, and the Zionist movement, which was bent on transforming the area into a Jewish state. We shall look in detail at the conflicts between Jewish and Arab nationalism in Palestine, and Britain's role in playing them off against each other, in chapters two and three. For the moment we only need to bear in mind that in July 1920 the mandate was used to replace the military government with a civil administration. The first High Commissioner, Sir Herbert Samuel, a British Jew sympathetic to the Zionists, opened the doors to massive Jewish immigration to Palestine: in the twenty years between 1920 and 1940 the Jewish population rose from 64,000 to 450,000. Growing Arab resistance and increasingly violent uprisings forced Britain into making drastic changes to its pro-Zionist policy. Of all the states created at this time Transjordan was without doubt the

most artificial. Having been included in the British zone by
the Sykes-Picot Agreement, it was incorporated into the
territories covered by the Palestinian mandate at the San
Remo conference, despite the cultural and traditional
differences separating the two countries. As early as 1921
Britain hived off Transjordan, creating an emirate and
putting Abdullah, the dethroned ruler of Iraq, on the
throne. The League of Nations ratified this partition in
1922, and excluded Transjordan from the provisions of
the mandate which related to the establishment of a Jewish
national homeland. In 1927 a treaty with Ibn Saud
guaranteed the southern border. Its status as a British
emirate was agreed by law and ratified by treaty in 1928.
The formal independence of Transjordan was not
declared until 1946.

Although Egypt had existed as a nation for centuries –
in contrast to the two preceding countries – the war served
to stimulate age-old nationalist opposition to British rule.
The whole inter-war period in Cairo was dominated by
complex manoeuvring involving the king, the British and
the nationalist Wafd Party. It started in 1919 when the
British deported the founder of the Wafd Party, Saad
Zaghlul, having refused to meet a delegation (Wafd, in
Arabic) led by him in November 1918. General Allenby
then called up reinforcements from Syria to assist in
breaking the general strike which followed. More trouble
occurred in 1921 and Zaghlul was deported again.
Although Britain conceded unilateral independence to
Egypt on 28 February 1922 it retained very considerable
control of communications and defence, and the
protection of foreign interests and national minorities in
both Egypt and Sudan. Sultan Fuad proclaimed himself
king on 15 March and promulgated a constitution to suit
himself in April. In the 1924 elections, however, the Wafd
won an overwhelming victory and Zaghlul, who became
prime minister, challenged Britain's privileged position.
Throughout the 1930s Fuad endeavoured to destroy the
power of the Wafd, appointing a strong man – Ishmael
Sidki – as prime minister, dissolving parliament, revoking
the constitution and engineering the election of an
assembly rendered meaningless by a Wafd boycott.

Popular unrest became so strong that in 1935 Fuad was forced to restore the constitution and come to terms with the nationalists. On 28 August 1936 his successor, Farouk, signed a new treaty with Britain which accorded enormous privileges to the British: the use of Egyptian facilities in the event of war and the right to station 10,000 troops in the Canal Zone to protect British interests, Egypt joined the League of Nations in 1937.

Although the Arabian peninsula was virtually untouched by the war, and the redistribution of territory which followed, a development took place there which was to fundamentally alter the picture: Sharif Hussein was replaced by Ibn Saud who set about unifying, under his leadership, the area which was to become Saudi Arabia. In January 1926 he was proclaimed king of the Hejaz. In the same year he concluded a treaty with Britain whereby his position as the completely independent King and leader of the Wahhabites was recognised. In exchange he agreed to recognise British territories in the Gulf and the border with Transjordan. In 1933, however, he granted a sixty year oil concession to Standard Oil of California, followed by a second one six years later, in spite of German and Japanese competition: this from a so-called 'friend' of Britain. This was the beginning of the long Saudi-American 'liaison'. North Yemen protected the independence it had acquired in 1918 by a series of alliances with Italy, the USSR, Britain, Holland and France, although its independent status was not formally recognised until it was admitted to the United Nations in 1947.

Elsewhere, all along the southern coast of the Arabian Peninsula and the Persian Gulf, Britain remained in control: Aden was still a British colony; a variety of treaties updated British 'protection' or 'supervision' of what are now South Yemen, Muscat and Oman, the Barbary Coast, Qatar, Bahrain and Kuwait. Britain's only competitor in the area was the United States, whose sole concern right up until the Second World War was to continue to acquire oil concessions. None of these states acquired independence until the 1960s and 1970s.

Unequal Shares

The Middle East saw a great deal of fighting during the First World War: the Dardanelles, Mesopotamia, Palestine, Sinai, Anatolia and Arabia were all battlefields at some time. The Second World War went on around the region rather than in it. The Axis powers tried to catch Britain in a pincer movement: from the Libyan desert in the west and through the Caucasus into Iraq in the north. Both of these offensives ultimately failed, the former thanks to the British army, assisted in the later stages by the American landings in North Africa, the latter thanks to the historic victory of the Red Army at Stalingrad. Nevertheless the global conflict had profound repercussions on the Middle East: there was a resurgence of Arab nationalism after a brief flirtation with the Axis powers; the United States began to take over Britain's predominant position in the area; while French influence all but disappeared. The problem of Palestine had to be resolved. The solution was to be partition; but only one new state was born – Israel.

In the eyes of the world the extermination of 6 million European Jews by the Nazis provided ample justification for the Zionist demand for a Jewish state. The Zionist cause benefitted to no small degree from justifiably strong guilt feelings in Europe and the United States about their responsibility for the genocide which had taken place. The story of the ship 'Exodus' and the cases of escapees from the camps who had been refused entry into or deported from Britain influenced public opinion in their favour. It proved a very strong factor in determining government policies.

It was decision time in Palestine: the stalemate had to end. The white paper published in 1939 was an important turning point in British policy: Jewish immigration was to be limited for five years and then left in the hands of the Arabs, land buying was to be restricted. The white paper foresaw the creation of a unified state within ten years, composed of one third Jews and two thirds Arabs, bound to Britain by a special treaty. It came after three years continual unrest in the area and was prompted by Britain's desire to win Arab support in the coming conflict with Hitler's Germany. In the aftermath of war, however, it became increasingly difficult to put the provisions of the white paper into practice. Clandestine Jewish immigration was taking place on an enormous scale, and increasing pressure came from pro-Zionists worldwide.

In 1943 the Stern Gang and the following year the Irgun group led by Menachem Begin began terrorist action in Palestine against British soldiers and property. In the aftermath of the attack on the King David Hotel on 22 July 1946, which claimed a hundred victims, the position of the new British Labour government became increasingly difficult as it faced condemnation from both Arabs and Zionists. Shaken by nationalist demonstrations and disturbances in Egypt and Iraq, the British government was determined to hold on to its position in Palestine, despite mounting international pressures, American demands and demonstrators in London chanting 'Bring the boys home'. 130 British soldiers were killed and 348 wounded in terrorist attacks between 1945 and the end of 1947.

After the failure of yet another round-table discussion the British Foreign Secretary, Bevin, announced on 14 February 1947 that the government had decided to take the whole issue to the United Nations. In May the U.N. set up a special commission, the U.N.S.C.O.P. (United Nations Special Committee on Palestine), to look into the different possibilities. With 650,000 Jews and 1,300,000 Arabs, any idea of a majority government drawn from one community only was out of the question. A bi-national state based on parity for each community was in theory the fairest possible solution and was supported by both the Communist Party of Palestine and left-wing Zionist groups, but the gulf between the two communities was so wide that the majority of Arabs and Jews rejected the idea of unity. The idea of dividing the territory into cantons was rejected on grounds of technical impracticality. Long-term international supervision would only serve to delay settlement of the issue. By a majority decision the UNSCOP voted to divide Palestine into three parts: a Jewish State, an Arab State, and a special zone under

The Expansion of Israel

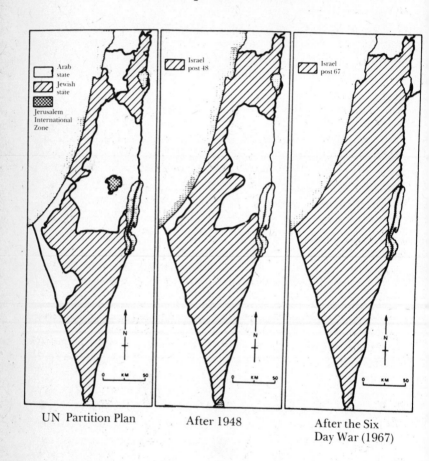

UN Partition Plan   After 1948   After the Six
                                            Day War (1967)

international supervision comprising the 'Holy Places' and the towns of Bethlehem and Jerusalem. A minority report came out in favour of a federation of Jewish and Arab states. The General Assembly of the United Nations sided with the majority report and agreed to partition on 29 November 1947.

The map on page 28 shows Palestine as it appeared after partition. The Jewish state comprised 14,000 square kilometres in Western Galilee, on the coastal strip between Acre and Ashod and in the Negev, with a population made up of 558,000 Jews and 405,000 Arabs. The Arab state comprised 11,500 square kilometres in Eastern Galilee, Samaria, the hills of Judea and the Gaza coastal strip, with a population made up of 804,000 Arabs and 10,000 Jews. The International Zone comprised 106,000 Arabs and 100,000 Jews. The two states were to form an economic union, with common currency, customs, railways and postal services in addition to joint administration of the ports of Haifa and Jaffa. Given these conditions it is not difficult to understand the marked lack of enthusiasm displayed by the U.N. and even by those who supported partition: one third of the population had been given more than half the territory, whereas in more than sixty years of 'colonisation' the Jews had only managed to buy 6.6% of the land.

But the planned partition never took place. Britain, after abstaining in the U.N. vote, decided to wreck it by announcing that it intended to give up its mandate before it expired on 15 May 1948. The British refused to hand over their powers and services to the International Commission designated by the U.N. They felt that the planned partition meant the end of the British presence in Palestine. The United States, supporting the Zionists, also hoped to prevent implementation of the partition agreement – despite having voted in favour of it. Yielding to British pressure, the Americans asked for the resolution to be annulled in March 1948. The Soviet Union alone continued to support the U.N. resolution, seeing it as the least unacceptable alternative. Andrei Gromyko told the U.N. on 14 May 1947 that 'the interests of both the Jews and the Arabs in Palestine can only be properly protected

by the creation of an Arab-Jewish state that is democratic
and independent, dual yet homogeneous'. But, he added,
'as a result of the increasingly strained relations between
Jews and Arabs', it was necessary to 'divide the country
into two independent states'. From November 1947
onwards the Soviet Union, mindful of imperialist
influence in the Middle East, saw the choice not as between
a unified state and partition but as between partition and a
continued British presence. The Arabs were solely
concerned with the danger of Zionism, and as allies of
Britain rejected the U.N. resolution.

The Zionists, meanwhile, were preparing for independence. The *Yishuv* had slowly become a nation, with
economic and political organisations, parties, institutions
and an army. A people's council was set up on 12 April
1948 which became the Provisional State Council on 14
May. On the day that the British mandate came to an end
the council declared that 'we by virtue of our natural and
historical right and of the resolution of the General
Assembly of the United Nations, do hereby proclaim the
creation of a Jewish state in the land of Israel'.

This meant independence, and with it came the first
Arab-Israeli conflict. Fighting had in fact started in 1947:
Arab attacks on the Jewish population, and armed Zionist
operations to occupy as much territory as possible, had
resulted in 350 deaths by December and some 2,000 by
March, following the infiltration into Palestine of the
'Arab Liberation Army'. Attacks perpetrated by the Irgun
and Stern terrorist gangs, aimed at forcing the Palestinians
out, reached appalling proportions: on 9 April 1948
Menachem Begin and his men massacred 250 elderly
people, women and children at Deir Yassin. Fighting
became more widespread in March and April following
the first Jewish victories, with Zionist troops seizing control
of the Arab towns of Jaffa and Acre. On 15 May 1948 the
armies of Transjordan, Egypt and Syria, assisted by Iraqi
and Lebanese troops, invaded Palestine. In replying to a
Wafd opponent, the Egyptian premier, Nokrashi Pasha,
revealed that the British had encouraged them to make
war. The conflict continued until 6 January 1949,
interrupted by truces which enabled Israel to stock up with

Czechoslovak arms. In this way the Soviet Union, which had recognised the existence of Israel *de jure* as early as 18 May 1948, made a major contribution to Israel's victory.

Israel and its different adversaries signed armistices between 23 February and 20 July 1949, which ratified the extension of the orders of the state of Israel by a third, as shown in the map on page 28. The chief outcome of the war, however, was the exile of hundreds of thousands of Palestinians. The U.N. counted 900,000 in Jordan, Gaza, Lebanon and Syria in April 1950. Their fight to return which was supported by a U.N. resolution in December 1948, was simply not accepted by the Israeli government. The government in fact was determined that the Palestinians should never return.

The Arab world came out of the conflict humiliated and destabilised. The Egyptian premier, Nokrashi Pasha, was assassinated in December 1948; the Wafd resumed power and in 1950 denounced the Anglo-Egyptian Treaty. The 'Free Officers' seized power on 23 July 1952. After riots at the end of 1948 Syria underwent one military coup after another. Iraq was also shaken by internal disorders. Transjordan was the only state to profit in any way from the conflict: secret agreements with the Zionist leaders enabled King Abdullah to annex the West Bank and to create the kingdom of Jordan on 24 April 1950. A year later he was assassinated in the Al Aqsa Mosque in Jerusalem.

America Takes Over

The traditional colonial powers' influence waned in the post-war period.

France had been expelled from the Levant in 1941. Following the Vichy government's surrender of Lebanon and Syria to the Axis, Britain, supported by Free French troops, had invaded both countries in July that year. Despite a declaration of independence issued by General de Gaulle's representative, General Catroux, French influence continued to decline, undermined by the nationalist movement, in which the Communists had a prominent role. Matters came to a head in Lebanon in

1943 and in Syria in 1944 when their parliaments revoked French 'privileges'. The 1945 invasion marked the beginning of the end for the French. As a result of British pressure, and the tacit consent of both the Soviet Union and the United States, Lebanon and Syria joined the international community without any reference to French interests, becoming founder members of the Arab League and the United Nations. After lengthy haggling, and under pressure from the U.N., French troops left the Levant. The last soldiers embarked at Beirut on 31 December 1946. Despite 'winning the war' British power had been seriously weakened, and now came under threat from the nationalist movement which held it responsible for the failure of Arab aspirations in Palestine. The British attempted to hold on to their position, establishing closer ties with sympathetic governments in the region and associating themselves with the Pan-Arab movement, but this only served to delay the inevitable. In the 50s Britain faced one setback after another: the nationalisation of the Anglo-Iranian Oil Company by Dr Mossadek in Iran in 1951, followed by the nationalisation of the Suez Canal in Egypt in 1956 and revolution in Iraq in 1958. British withdrawal from the Middle East culminated in the decision forced on the government in 1967 to end all involvement in the area east of Suez, which led to the independence of Aden and the Gulf states.

The United States, whose forces had only been involved in a small way in the fighting in the region during the Second World War, now did very well out of the situation. American economic and strategic interests came to the fore at the expense of their British ally. The most significant element was oil: American oil production in the region went up from 13.9% of the total in 1938 to 55.2% in 1948, a period in which total output had risen threefold. This area, bordering the Soviet Union, assumed a major geopolitical significance for Washington at the beginning of the cold war. Using the so-called 'point four' of the 1949 Economic Assistance Law, the United States government authorised the payment of hundreds of millions of dollars to Arab countries. Propaganda was handled by the local offices of the United States Information Service, which

soon became targets for Arab nationalists. President
Truman states in his memoirs that this programme was in
accordance with the US policy of preventing marxist
expansion in the free world by helping to ensure the right
sort of development. Its aim was to give hope for people
threatened by 'communist propaganda'. The main aim of
both American and British policy, however, was to create
an Anti-Soviet pact. The main problem lay in convincing
the Arabs that the real threat came not from Tel Aviv but
from Moscow – a difficulty not unknown in later days to
Kissinger, Haig and Schultz.

The history of this strategy, which has never really
worked, is too long and too complex to be gone into here.
In 1950 it took the form of a tripartite declaration in which
the United States, Britain and France undertook to
guarantee the frontiers agreed in the Middle East by the
Armistice against any threatened violation. In 1951
Greece and Turkey were invited to join NATO, and in
November of that year the Supreme Allied Command for
the Middle East was born, uniting America, Britain,
France and Turkey. After American intervention in Iran
to overthrow Mossadek in 1953 three more 'successes'
were chalked up in 1954: the Turko-Pakistani colla-
boration agreement, Iraq's decision to accept American
aid, which it had hitherto rejected, and a new
Anglo-Egyptian agreement on Suez. The beginning of
1955 was marked by the Turko-Iraqi mutual co-operation
pact, known as the Baghdad pact, to which Britain,
followed by Pakistan and Iran, also adhered. The British
government hoped it would also include the Arab
countries, but Lebanon, Jordan, Egypt and Syria all
refused to join, and in fact resistance to the Baghdad pact
was to give added impetus and cohesion to the nationalist
movement of which Nasser was to be the figurehead for
fifteen years.

Suez: the Boomerang

The effect of western policies was to boost nationalism,
neutrality and hostility towards Israel in the Arab world.
The unscrupulous pillage of the resources of these

countries strengthened the desire for independence and increased people's awareness of their exploitation. The West's obsessive anti-sovietism and consequent desire to impose anti-soviet defence pacts on the Arabs rebounded in one of two ways: either by resulting in Arab non-alignment in East-West affairs or, worse still from a Western point of view, by the creation of Arab alliances with the Soviet Union. As the rapprochement between Israel and the West became more apparent these tendencies were accentuated. Israel's first foreign minister, Moshe Sharett, favoured non-alignment and cultivated good relations with the Soviet Union which, as we have seen, had made a significant contribution to the creation of the Jewish state and to the defeat of its Arab neighbours. By way of illustration we can point to the common reaction of the USSR and Israel to the Chinese revolution – both recognised the People's Democratic Republic – and to their attitude towards Spain, where they both opposed lifting the boycott on Franco's regime. Both sides bear responsibility for the deterioration in relations which followed, but the main fault lies with the Soviet Union. When the Israeli ambassador to the Soviet Union, Golda Meyerson – later to change her name to Meir – attended Jewish New Year celebrations at the synagogue in September 1948 she was welcomed so enthusiastically by Soviet Jews that the Kremlin became worried. The Soviet leadership was and remains concerned about the influence of Zionism on the millions of Jews in the Soviet Union. 1949 saw the start of the 'anti-zionist' purges which culminated in the Stalinist show trials of the post-war period. Israel, meanwhile, was moving closer to the West. In 1950 Ben Gurion sided with the West over Korea and the next year sought a military alliance with the United States. While on an official visit to Britain and the United States he offered them the use of Israeli harbours and airports. Relations with the Soviet Union were broken off in 1953, and were not resumed until after the death of Stalin. In 1955 Ben Gurion offered the Americans military bases in return for a guarantee of Israel's borders.

In Arab eyes all parties were compromised by this

'flirtation': the West was seen as unilaterally pro-Israeli, while Israel, having annexed Jerusalem and declared it the capital of the country in 1949 despite U.N. opposition, continued to refuse to abide by the U.N. instruction to allow the refugees to return. Increasingly bloody reprisals followed border incidents such as those at Kibya on the frontier with Jordan in 1953 and in Gaza Strip in 1955. Secret indirect negotiations between Nasser and Sharett, who had become prime minister at the end of 1953, came to nothing after Ben Gurion returned to power in 1955. So, while the West was accused of countenancing and even actively supporting Israeli intransigence, Israel itself appeared to be no more than a puppet in Western hands. The Arab world united against these two enemies who in their eyes were inextricably linked.

In 1955 the Bandung conference witnessed the birth of what was later to be called the Non-Aligned Movement. One of its father figures, and one of the first to put its principles into practice, was Gamal Abdul Nasser. When the West announced in September that they would only supply arms to Arab countries on the understanding that they would not be used against Israel, Nasser responded by stating that he would arrange to purchase what he wanted from Czechoslovakia. After the Israeli raid on Gaza at the beginning of the year which claimed many casualties Egypt felt the need to build up its defences. As a counter to the Baghdad pact Egypt and Syria signed a military pact in October, soon to be joined by Saudi Arabia, who saw it as a means of furthering their longstanding opposition to the Hashemites. The combined forces of the three countries were placed under the leadership of the Egyptian general Abdel Hakim Amer. Preparations were completed the next year with the signing of a military pact between Egypt, Saudi Arabia and Yemen. On 26 July 1956 Nasser announced the nationalisation of the Suez canal. The United States had finally refused to finance the construction of the Aswan dam, so the resources of the nationalised Canal Company would be used instead. The repercussions of this action went far beyond Egypt and the Middle East: it was the first time, other than the Iranian nationalisation of the oil companies which had in any case been rescinded, that a third world country had sought to regain control of its natural resources.

This was too much for Israel and Britain, as well as for France which saw an opportunity to make up for its disastrous failures in North Africa. At the secret conference of Sevres on 23 October plans were made for military intervention in Egypt. The Israelis had for some time made it clear that any military alliance between Egypt, Syria and Jordan would constitute a *casus belli*. On 24 October the Jordanian assembly, which had only been elected four days previously, and in which Baathists and Communists held the majority, voted to join the Syro-Saudi-Yemeni-Egyptian alliance.

The second Arab-Israeli war began on 29 October. In the space of six days the Israeli army swept through and occupied Sinai, capturing 6,000 Egyptian soldiers and 100 T34 tanks. On 30 October Britain and France presented an ultimatum to Egypt and Israel, demanding that they evacuate the canal zone. It was rejected by the government in Cairo the following day, at which point the British and French governments ordered the bombing of Egyptian targets. Despite a U.N. ceasefire order dated 1 November the fighting continued to escalate: British and French troops disembarked at Port Said and Ismailia on 5 November. Only strong American pressure and Soviet threats were able to force the British and French to abide by the U.N. injunction. Their forces evacuated Port Said on 22 December; Israeli forces did not pull out of Sinai until 14 March 1957.

It was, then, a total fiasco. Israel achieved nothing except the stationing of U.N. observers in the Gaza Strip and at Sharm Al Shaikh, which ensured freedom of navigation in the Gulf of Aqaba and access to the port of Eilat. For Britain and France it was worse still: not only was the Suez canal blocked, cutting off oil supplies, but the international status of both countries, which had already been on the decline in the region, now reached an all-time low. On 13 November the Arab heads of state, with the exception of Lebanon, cut off diplomatic relations with France. The French also had to contend with insurrectionists in Algeria, for whom the humiliation of France in Egypt acted as a great morale booster. Britain's treaties with Jordan and Egypt were abrogated. The traditional colonial powers had lost out. The time was ripe for an American take-over.

American prestige had been untarnished by the Suez affair. Although critical of the nationalisation of the Suez canal the Americans had nevertheless opposed the Franco-British intervention and sought to bring it to an end. However, the so-called Eisenhower Doctrine, as laid out by the President on 5 January 1957, served only to confirm Arab suspicions of the imperialist 'Uncle Sam' role of the United States. Although couched in terms of economic co-operation and military assistance Eisenhower made no attempt to conceal the real objectives of American policy: the defence of the Middle East against Soviet 'power politics' and the global ambitions of world communism. Pointing to the Soviet bogey was not enough to allay Arab concern over the position of Israel; the new American proposals on Israel were contrary to the provisions of the Baghdad Pact. The only countries to accept the American overtures were Lebanon, under Chamoun, Iraq, under Nuri Said, and Saudi Arabia. In these countries and elsewhere the aftermath of Suez was brutal, there were riots in Iraq, for example. In Egypt Nasser nationalised British and French companies and released left-wing prisoners. In Syria the Baathist-Communist coalition had been leaning towards Moscow since June 1955: now, as the United States, Turkey, Lebanon, Iraq and Israel became increasingly hostile, the government in Damascus responded by establishing closer ties with Moscow. Soviet ships and Egyptian troops backed up the Syrian regime. This process culminated on 1 February 1958 with the declaration of the unification of Egypt and Syria and the formation of the United Arab Republic. On 14 July of the same year a revolution took place in Iraq in which both the king and Nuri Said lost their lives, and General Kassem took charge. The ensuing panic was so widespread that on the following day American marines occupied Beirut, where civil war against Chamoun was raging, and British parachutists occupied Amman. Faced with the danger of the contagion spreading the Pentagon must have thought it better to take action to prevent another war.

Thus the Suez affair had a boomerang effect. It was aimed at nipping in the bud the growth of nationalism and neutrality, but in fact it stimulated both. The United States, taking over from Britain and France in the Middle East, proceeded to make the same mistakes. American determination to involve the Arabs in their anti-soviet 'crusade', their growing support for Israel, their aid to unpopular regimes and their grotesque caricature of Nasser – who had been ready to negotiate with them – all contributed to stirring up hatred against them throughout the region. After the war in Indochina Suez marked the beginning of a new chapter in history. Peoples and states of the Third World would no longer allow themselves to be pushed around by the industrialised countries; they would come to play a leading role in deciding the course of human history.

Six Days That Shook The World

In many ways the third Arab-Israeli war was like the second. It was started by Israel in an attempt to restrain the rising tide of Arab liberation. The pretexts were identical: the closure of the Gulf of Aqaba and above all the Jordanian decision to join the Syro-Egyptian Pact. The Israeli offensive went on for the same length of time and again culminated in overwhelming military victory for Israel. But there were three major differences between the 56 war and the 67 war: on this occasion Israel fought alone, although with considerable American support in terms of hardware; it fought on three fronts instead of one; and, most importantly, this time the occupied territories were not handed back. In the space of six days in June 1967 the state of Israel quadrupled in size.

The Arab world did not experience a steady process of development in the 60s, but considerable progress did take place: in Algeria independence was achieved after eight years of heroic struggle; the Egyptian regime became more radical; a republican revolution took place in North Yemen; in Aden armed struggle began against the British;

in Syria a coalition of Baathists and Communists came to power in 1966. On the other hand a large number of setbacks and defeats also took place: in 1963 a very bloody witch-hunt followed the removal of Kassem in Iraq, where fighting with the Kurds had started two years previously; Egypt got involved in Yemen as a counter to Saudi support for the royalists; more and more confrontations occurred in Jordan between the army and the Palestinians. The bright spots of 'Arab socialism' remained few and far between.

Baathism, already in power in Syria and soon to be so in Iraq, is a movement that reflects this difficult situation. Founded in the 40s as a nationalist movement set on unifying the Arab world it had split into mutually antagonistic national sections. It embodied the aspirations of the urban petty bourgeoisie whose radicalism had come out of their conflict with imperialism; they were noticably reluctant to see the wholesale transformation of society.

The context in which the sudden increase in tension between the Arabs and their Hebrew neighbour occurred was Israel's unilateral decision in 1963 to divert the waters of the River Jordan. In mid-January 1964 there was a summit of Arab heads of state in Cairo – the first of its kind. They responded to Israel's action by diverting the waters of two of three rivers that form the Jordan, thereby reducing it by half. An armed force under General Amer was put in charge of protecting the engineering works which went on despite Israeli reprisals. The same summit witnessed the first steps towards the concept of a 'Palestinian entity' when Ahmed Shukeiri was given the task of forming the Palestine Liberation Organisation and the Palestine Liberation Army. The Al Fatah movement, jumping the gun, so to speak, with Syrian backing, infiltrated some of its commandos into Israel via Jordan in January 1965.

The build-up for the next war had started. More and more incidents occurred. These were interspersed with bloody Israeli raids into Jordan and Syria which inflicted heavy casualties in 'reprisal' for the work being done to alter the course of the River Jordan and for the attacks of Yasser Arafat's organisation. Israeli leaders' memoirs for

this period show that the military was busily preparing a
pre-emptive strike against the progressive Arab states at
this time. In April 1967 both Cairo and Damascus were
worried about the possibility of invasion. Their fears grew
following an Israeli military parade in Jerusalem on 15
May, in open breach of the armistice agreement. The
Egyptian army was put on the alert two days later. On the
18th Nasser called for the withdrawal of United Nations
observers from the Gaza Strip and Sharm Al Shaikh.
Egyptian soldiers took possession of both on the 21st and
the next day closed the Gulf of Aqaba to Israeli ships and
to ships bound for Israel carrying strategically important
goods. The Interministerial Defence Committee met in
Tel Aviv, with Moshe Dayan and Shimon Peres sitting
down with Menachem Begin – who had joined the
government for the first time on 1 June. The day before
King Hussein of Jordan had joined the Syro-Egyptian
military pact, followed by Iraq on 4 June. A few hours
later the Israeli armed forces attacked: the Arab air forces
were wiped out in the space of a few hours that morning;
Sinai and the West Bank were occupied within six days.
Egypt and Syria accepted the United Nations ceasefire
instruction on the 8th, but Israel continued to advance for
another two days, by which time her forces had gained
control of the Golan Heights.

With the benefit of hindsight the flood of pro-Israeli
propaganda which inundated France at the time now
seems literally scandalous: it must be said that the
Communists were almost alone in not spreading the myth
of the Israeli David facing up to the Arab Goliath, and in
not yielding to the anti-Arab racism which was widespread
in the aftermath of the French humiliation in Algeria.
History has overlooked these lies, and people continue to
believe them. Yet there is no longer even one creditable
Israeli leader who is prepared to deny that the
overwhelming superiority of their armed forces meant
that Israel was never in any real danger, even if they are
not prepared to admit that the attacks on Egypt, Syria and
Jordan were premeditated. General Rabin who was Chief
of Staff at the time and therefore responsible for starting
the war made the following statement to the daily

newspaper *Haaretz* on 19 March 1972: 'I don't think Nasser wanted war. The two divisions he sent into Sinai on 14 May wouldn't have been enough to launch an offensive against Israel. He knew it and we knew it'. General Peled, who it is true has since become a pacifist, said on the same day 'The thesis that genocide was hanging over our heads in June 1967 and that Israel was fighting for its very existence was just pure bluff'.

A War For Peace

Like the 1948 debacle the 1967 disaster destabilised the Arab world. Although the regimes survived, developments began within them which came to the surface in the 70s. Broadly speaking the Arab nationalist movement had carried out its antifeudal and anticolonial tasks, with the significant exception of the Palestinian question. Its decline was part of a social change which had been gradually taking place over many years. An increasingly bitter struggle was taking place between the bureaucratic, agricultural and commercial bourgeoisie on the one hand and the interests of the lower classes as voiced in part by the communist parties and large sections of the nationalist parties on the other. The issues at stake in this conflict were agrarian reform, social progress, the nature of industrial development, democracy, the role of the working class and regional and international alliances. The contradictory developments in Middle Eastern affairs result from these tensions.

In Egypt Anwar Al Sadat, who took over after Nasser's death on 28 September 1970, opened the way to economic 'liberalisation' and broke off ties with the Soviet Union after expelling about 20,000 Soviet experts and advisers in July 1972. In Syria Hafez Assad seized power in November 1970, removed the left-wing Baathists and also announced a policy of '*infitah*' or economic opening towards the capitalist world. In Iraq on the other hand Hassan Al Bakr, Sadam Hussein and the Baathists moved towards a rapprochement with the Soviet Union after a coup in July 1968 and in 1971-2 came to terms with the communists at home. This marked the high point of Soviet influence in the Middle East, which had benefitted from the failure of the Baghdad pact and the Eisenhower doctrine. Arab nationalism achieved successes in Libya, where the monarchy succumbed to a coup led by Gadhafi in September 1969, and on the coasts of the Arabian Peninsula. British troop withdrawals from Aden in 1967 and then from the Gulf Emirates finally led to independence. In contrast an ultra-left putsch in Sudan was put down in a bloodbath in July 1971. Among those killed were the leaders of the powerful Sudanese Communist Party. The adventurism of the Popular Front for the Liberation of Palestine (P.F.L.P.) under George Habash and the Democratic Front for the Liberation of Palestine (D.F.L.P.) under Nayef Hawatmeh finally gave King Hussein of Jordan the excuse he had been waiting for to crush the Palestinian resistance in 'Black' September 1970, the first of many stabs in the back for the P.L.O.

The Jewish state profited from these contradictory tendencies in order to establish its supremacy and to put an early end to any peace plans. The Tel Aviv government annexed the old city of Jerusalem as early as July 1967 and refused to permit the return of 200,000 new refugees who had fled during the war: 20,000 only were allowed to go back to their homes. The first Jewish settlements in the West Bank began. Anti-Palestinian repression – using the same emergency law which the Zionists had called Nazi in 1945 when the British had used it against them – increased steadily. U.N. resolution 242, which had taken the Security Council five months of complex wrangling to reach, was rejected out of hand by Tel Aviv. It included the withdrawal of Israeli forces from the occupied territories, ending the state of war, recognition of all the states in the region, freedom of navigation on the Suez canal and in the Gulf of Aqaba and the creation of demilitarised zones. Although the Arab summit in Khartoum at the end of August 1967 had said no to negotiation, Nasser and Husein had left the door open. Israel closed it.

The same happened to all subsequent attempts at reaching a settlement. Egypt's sit and wait strategy over the Suez canal forced the United States, after consultation with the Soviet Union, to draw up the Rogers plan in July

1970. The basic idea was to work out a timetable for the implementation of Resolution 242. Once Egypt and Jordan had agreed to the appointment of Jarring as the mediator to take on this task Israel was forced to do likewise, which led to the downfall of the Likud government. It must be pointed out that the sit and wait policy was extremely damaging both for the Egyptian towns along the canal and for Israeli morale. Yet in September Tel Aviv broke off negotiations. The only lasting effect of this episode was a canal zone ceasefire which continued until 1973. Sadat took the initiative again in December 1970, presenting a peace plan in which Israel would be recognised in exchange for the return of the occupied territories, and freedom of navigation on the Suez Canal would be guaranteed in exchange for the return of Palestinian refugees. Once again Tel Aviv turned a deaf ear to the proposals: the occupied territories formed part of Israel's 'secure' frontiers, even though the Israeli government refused to define these frontiers. The same response greeted the Nixon-Brezhnev joint declaration of May 1972 in which they reaffirmed their commitment to a peaceful solution conforming to Resolution 242, and their wish to contribute to the success of the Jarring Mission.

The Arab Leaders and Sadat in particular were by now convinced that the only way to force the Soviet Union, and more especially the United States, to apply all the 'arguments' at their disposal in order to bring Israel to the negotiating table was by another war. The Egyptian leader was all the more sure of this because of popular demonstrations at home against his inaction. Displaying all the talents of which Israeli leaders were past masters he made it clear, despite general disbelief, that Egypt was preparing for war. 'There is no more hope of a peaceful agreement. We have decided to fight', he said in November 1971. Finally, in March 1973, Sadat assumed the role of Prime Minister as well as President 'in the light of a total confrontation with Israel'.

It happened on 6 October, the day of the Jewish feast of Kippur. Egyptian troops crossed the Suez Canal and swept through the fortified Bar Lev line, while Syrian soldiers

penetrated the Golan Heights front to a distance of five
kilometres. It was already a historical victory: the Arab
armies had avenged the defeats of 1948, 1956 and 1967.
The myth of the invincibility of the armed forces was
destroyed. It took the Israeli generals a week to get a grip
on things, thanks partly to Sadat's decision to halt his
offensive. On 12 October Israeli tanks broke through on
the Golan Heighs and in Sinai, where a certain General
Sharon crossed the canal and headed for Suez in breech of
orders from headquarters. In the west the Israeli
bridgehead grew larger. One of the most impressive tank
battles of the century took place on 17 October in the Sinai
Desert. On the same day in Kuwait the Organisation of
Arab Petroleum Exporting Countries, (O.A.P.E.C.), the
Arab O.P.E.C., declared an oil embargo: the first oil crisis
began. On the 22nd Security Council Resolution 338 was
agreed by Egypt and Israel. The armed forces however
did not respect the ceasefire the next day. It took a Soviet
threat to send troops to the area, followed by the
American response of putting their troops on third degree
military alert, to induce Tel Aviv to respect the ceasefire.
Hostilities eventually came to an end on 24 October 1973.

Missed Opportunities

Sadat hoped to achieve peace by waging war. For a while
after the October war it seemed that he was right. Israel
underwent a crisis during which the very nature of the
'Arab policy' followed by successive governments since the
creation of the Hebrew state was brought into question:
the doves became more numerous and more influential.
The Arab countries, meanwhile, flush with their military
successes, adopted a more realistic approach to the
problem of finding a lasting solution to the conflict. For
the time being at least Washington and Moscow saw eye to
eye about the need to resolve the problems in the region
without recourse to another war which would be both
ruinous and dangerous to world stability: this was the
heyday of detente. Europe agreed, prompted by the threat
of an O.P.E.C. oil embargo on pro-Israeli countries.
Regardless of their position vis-à-vis Zionism the old

western metropolitan countries had to get used to the discomfort of paying realistic prices for the petroleum products which they had once taken as a matter of course. To all intents and purposes the only element needed before an equitable peace settlement could be reached was the agreement of the Israeli leadership. This was not forthcoming, for in Tel Aviv the hawks were in the ascendant, in the guise both of the Labour Party and, following the elections in 1977, the reactionary coalition led by Menachem Begin. Faced with this immovable object Egypt, worn out by carrying the heaviest burden in the conflict, gave up trying to bring about global negotiations and agreed to a separate peace agreement.

And yet it was not so much a case of there not being any opportunities for making peace after the Yom Kippur war as that the opportunities that did exist were missed. In December 1973 a Geneva conference, jointly chaired by Andrei Gromyko and Henry Kissinger, brought together representatives of Israel, Egypt and Jordan; but when the Israelis rejected any idea of making concessions over the occupied territories it was adjourned. The question of the role of the P.L.O. in the talks got in the way of any possible resumption. Meanwhile an Israeli-Egyptian peace settlement came steadily nearer: Henry Kissinger's one-step-at-a-time policy resulted in the November 1973 'kilometre 101' agreement and in January 1974 the complete withdrawal from the canal zone. It proved to be much more difficult to achieve, but eventually the same strategy resulted in a Syrian-Israeli disengagement agreement on the Golan Heights.

Basking in these glorious achievements the United States decided to go it alone and achieve some form of *pax americana* without reference to either the Soviet Union or the U.N. In June 1974 Richard Nixon went on a tour of Arab capitals and Jerusalem. But another year was to go by, during which, incidentally, civil war began in Lebanon, before the next Israeli-Egyptian agreement was signed on 1 September 1975. This marked the end of the state of war between the two countries, who undertook not to use force in future. Egypt agreed to lift the sea blockade and even opened the Suez Canal to Israeli shipping. Israel withdrew to a distance of 50 kilometres from the canal and handed back the Sinai oilfields. A demilitarised zone was created in which U.N. troops took up position. This agreement had within it the seeds of the Camp David accords: Israel was ready to withdraw from Egyptian territory in order to reach a separate peace agreement but was not, and would not be, prepared to concede anything on the issue of the rights of the Palestinians.

Another opportunity was missed in December 1976. The General Assembly of the U.N. called Israel, Egypt, Jordan and Syria to take part in an international conference. The new American president, Jimmy Carter, laid down three preconditions: firstly, recognition of the existence of Israel; secondly, the negotiation of permanent frontiers; lastly – and for the first time – the Palestinian right to a 'homeland'. The Israeli Labour prime minister Yitzhak Rabin categorically rejected these preconditions, as did his successor Menachem Begin: on 17 May 1977 the Right had won an electoral victory in Israel for the first time since 1948. The consequences of this victory soon became apparent: the Geneva conference got bogged down, there was a marked increase in new Jewish settlements in 'Judea and Samaria', Gaza and Sinai, and more raids on Lebanon. The Soviet Union played its last card on 1 October 1977 when Gromyko and the American secretary of state Cyrus Vance jointly signed a declaration calling on all parties to return to the negotiating table in Geneva on the basis of U.N. Resolution 242, and the legitimate rights of the Palestinian people. It was too late. The White House soon abandoned that strategy and concentrated all its energies on Begin and Sadat.

In his autobiography, *In Search of Identity*, the Egyptian president argues by way of self-justification that they had to find 'a completely new approach that would bypass all formalities and procedural technicalities by pulling down the barrier of mutual mistrust. Only thus ... could we hope to break out of the vicious circle and avert the blind alley of the past'. On 19 November 1977 the world was astonished to learn that Sadat was in Jerusalem. Unfortunately his unprecedented historic gesture was not reciprocated: although the Egyptian leader eventually left out any reference to the P.L.O. in his speech to the Knesset, Begin simply delivered an intolerant exhortation without any gesture whatsoever towards the Palestinians.

A final opportunity was missed when Sadat returned to Cairo. The international conference which Sadat had suggested as a way forward from Geneva never took place. In December Libya, Syria, the P.L.O., Algeria and the Democratic Republic of Yemen came together to form an uncompromising front against 'Egyptian treachery'. The Soviet Union supported them. The Egyptian president responded by saying 'I will go all the way down the path of negotiations even if the other Arab countries refuse to come with me'.

Less than a year later, after moments of tension which nearly brought about a break in relations between Israel and Egypt, Jimmy Carter got what he wanted. He invited Begin and Sadat to Camp David, where they signed two accords on 17 September 1978. One dealt with the drawing up of a peace treaty between the two countries. This treaty was to be signed within three months. It included recognition of Egypt's sovereignty over Sinai and an undertaking by Israel to withdraw her troops within two or three years. Normal relations, and more particularly diplomatic relations, were to be established. The second accord drew up a framework of peace in the Middle East, and dealt chiefly with the occupied territories. Negotiations involving Israel, Egypt and Jordan were to create an 'autonomous' area incorporating the West Bank and Gaza, after which a transitional phase of five years was planned: what would happen then remained rather vague. The Israeli-Egyptian accord was the only one which came to anything: the peace treaty was signed in Washington, later than intended, on 26 March 1979; and following the dismantling of the last Jewish settlements, Sinai reverted to Egyptian sovereignty on 25 April 1982. By contrast, the second accord has not, up until now, shown anything other than superficial signs of life.

The Camp David accords did not lead to a global peace settlement for four reasons. As separate agreements they only involved one of the Arab countries concerned, albeit the most powerful one; neither the other countries nor the representatives of the Palestinians, who were at the heart of the problem from the outset, took part in the discussions preceding the agreements. The accords were in two parts yet nothing in them required them to be applied simultaneously: Israel could demand that Egypt abide by the treaty while Egypt could not other than formally require action to be taken to set up the 'autonomous' Palestinian area which the Cairo government thought would precede self-determination for the Palestinian people. It should be stated that the accords were signed with a partner whose duplicity was quite stunning: the ink was hardly dry on the paper before Begin made Israel's position crystal clear: no to a return to pre-1967 borders; no to reverting to an Arab Jerusalem; no to a Palestinian state in Gaza and the West Bank. Furthermore he authorised an increase in the very settlements he had pledged to dismantle. It must also be pointed out that Camp David came into being under American auspices only, without any reference to the Soviet Union, whereas the history of the Middle East has shown that if there is to be a stable and lasting outcome of the Arab-Israeli conflict it can only be achieved with the joint approval of both of the great powers.

Reckless Actions

The separate peace treaty concluded between Israel and Egypt was not just useless; it acted as a stimulus to a government which, finding itself in a position of strength, now plunged itself into reckless action which had very worrying consequences. The Tel Aviv administration had never before had so much elbow room for expansionism in the Middle East.

Egypt had isolated itself. The Arab embassies in Cairo were shut, the offices of the Arab League transferred to Tunis. Economic sanctions were imposed. The Arab world, thus weakened, became more divided than ever. After a brief respite tension built up again between Damascus and Baghdad. The Iranian revolution lost its soul in a bloody conflict with Iraq which had attacked Iran after the break-up of an alliance. The Iraqi Baathists had broken up the National Front and hounded out the communists. For a while it seemed that Syria and Jordan were on the brink of war. The Western Sahara affair served to revive old animosities in the Maghreb. The special relationship that most of these countries and the Gulf states had with the United States rendered them powerless to resist Israel. The positive proposals from the 1978 Baghdad Summit aimed at a global solution to the conflict were just words.

Israel, having settled things on its southern flank, was now free to set about doing the same on its northern flank in order to 'settle' the Palestinian problem. Bolstered by another election victory in 1981 the Likud had at its disposal all the means it required to launch an all-out assault. With the 'autonomy' negotiations with Egypt blocked, new settlers rapidly extended the colonisation of the West Bank and the Gaza Strip. Jerusalem was 'reunified' and proclaimed capital of Israel in June 1980. The number of settlements rose from 24 in 1977 to 108 in 1983, the number of settlers from 3,200 to 25,000, not counting the 80,000 Jews in the Jerusalem area. As repression continued the Palestinians continued to demonstrate, major rioting breaking out at the end of 1979, in May 1980, June 1981, and in March and April 1982 after a number of democratically elected mayors were removed from office.

This aggression went beyond Israel's borders: Syria was one target, at the time of the 'missile crisis' in the spring of 1981 and again on 14 December that year when the Knesset decreed the annexation of the Golan Heights, whose Druze population organised a lengthy strike in protest. The sword of Damocles fell on Iraq on 7 June 1981 when nine Israeli jets destroyed the nuclear power station at Tamuz even though it was run by the International Energy Agency. The armed forces also violated Saudi air space in November 1981.

It was in Lebanon, however, that Israeli belligerence was demonstrated most thoroughly: making the most of the splits between the different Lebanese factions, and between the Lebanese and the Palestinians, the Israelis slowly increased their hold over the country with raid after raid. The first big military intervention, the Litani operation, began on 15 March 1978. On the 11th a Palestinian commando squad had taken hostage an Israeli bus, on the road from Haifa to Tel Aviv. On the pretence of seeking revenge 30,000 Israeli soldiers invaded Southern Lebanon: fighting with the Palestinians and the Lebanese national forces dragged on for nearly three months. The armed forces withdrew but handed over the job of 'protecting' nearly 1,000 square kilometres of territory to Lebanese mercenaries under the command of Saad Haddad. For the next three years a running battle continued. Lebanese towns and Palestinian camps were bombed by the Israeli air force, and commando raids and small scale invasions took place. In the words of the Beirut government Israel was systematically 'eating away' at Lebanon. The second big flare-up occurred in July 1981. Furious fighting between Palestinian and Israeli forces came to an end on the 25th as a result of an American-arranged ceasefire between the P.L.O. and Israel. Although the guns were silent for the next eleven months it was supposedly in defence of the 'peace of Galilee' that Israel launched the invasion of Lebanon on 6 June 1982. Initially announced by Menachem Begin, with the approval of Shimon Peres, as an operation that would go no more than 40 kilometres into Lebanon, in fact the Israeli army pressed on as far as Beirut. The Lebanese capital was under siege. The Palestinians, who had forced Israel to fight the longest war in her history, left on board U.N. ships. After Yasser Arafat had left with the last of his fighters on 30 August, General Sharon's troops entered the ruins of West Beirut. On 17 September the Phalangists carried out the massacres at Sabra and Shatila under the protection of the Israeli armed forces. Hundreds of victims had their throats cut or their guts ripped out, and were added to the 20,000 dead and 30,000 wounded on the Lebanese and Palestinian side of the fifth Arab-Israeli conflict. In the process of waging the war the Israeli forces used phosphorous bombs, napalm bombs, fragmentation bombs and even implosion bombs. Public opinion, faced with this horrifying spectacle, was traumatised. For the very first time in Israeli history tens of thousands of Israelis demonstrated against the war in Tel Aviv and Jerusalem, as did many Jews in the diaspora. The Arab peoples were stunned by this catastrophe, which their governments had allowed to happen. European and American public opinion which had traditionally been overwhelmingly pro-Israeli was shocked and conscience-stricken. After Beirut nothing would ever be the same again.

Chapter 2

Israel: From Certainty to Doubt

As Israel entered into 1984, it was breaking records. Inflation was touching on 300%, unemployment, which had hitherto been kept under control, was on the verge of trebling, the most heavily indebted country in the world seemed likely to incur still more debt, etcetera, etcetera. Things were so bad that it was probable that the Likud would be beaten at the next elections as a consequence of the collapse of consensus politics. The Jewish state and Zionism in general had been shaken by a crisis of identity which was reflected in the announcement of unprecedentedly high emigration figures – which some people put as high as 50,000. The strongest economic, political and military power in the Middle East had been rocked to its foundations.

But we need to do more than just look at the state of affairs of Israel in the 1980s. To understand present day Israel we have to go right back to its origins in Zionism and in the establishment of the *Yishuv* – the Jewish community in Palestine – in order to trace the roots of the mass of contradictions which go to make up the state of Israel.

Next Year in Jerusalem

The state of Israel is unique for two reasons. It is the only country born out of an ideology, where the people are 'selected', largely from within the Zionist movement, so linking them on a permanent basis to millions of Jews all over the world. It is also the only country created by a U.N. Resolution.

Zionism must therefore be included in any analysis of Israel and the Middle East, not just from a theoretical point of view but in order to understand how it has inspired and strengthened the determination of hundreds of thousands of people.

For generations of Jews the psalmist's incantation 'Next year in Jerusalem' served to keep alive the memory of Zion – the hill in Jerusalem that represented the promised land in allegorical form – and the hope that one day they would 'return' there. Following the destruction of the Jewish kingdoms at the hands of first the Assyrians and then the Babylonians, the Roman suppression of the Bar Kokhba revolt in 135 A.D. led to the general dispersion, or diaspora, of the Hebrews. Only a very small Jewish community remained in Palestine. The Jewish communities in Jerusalem, Safed, Tiberias and Hebron lived on the charitable gifts (*halukka*) of Jews in the diaspora, particularly from the eighteenth century onwards. As time went by a few pilgrims came to swell their meagre ranks, and then, at the end of the fifteenth century, a considerable number of Jews arrived there who had been expelled from the Iberian peninsula. Numerous 'messiahs' came along, from David Alroy in the twelfth century to Sabbatai Zevi in the eighteenth century, all of them proclaiming the resurrection of the Holy Land as predicted in the holy books. In 1835 there were 10,000 Jews in Palestine.

The religious idea was transformed into a political commitment to the rebirth of Israel during the eighteenth and nineteenth centuries. In the middle of the Egyptian campaign Napoleon had exhorted the Jews 'to flock to our colours and re-establish the old city of Jerusalem'. Byron and Disraeli in Britain, Napoleon III's secretary and the followers of Saint-Simon in France, all lent their weight to the cause. The first pre-Zionists appeared: amongst the more notable were the German Moses Hess, a former ally of Marx and Engels, who published *Rome and Jerusalem* in 1862, and the Russian Leon Pinsker whose book *Self-determination* led to the setting up of the Lovers of Zion group, which organised the first emigration to Palestine. Colonisation of the 'bible lands' began. In 1880 there were

25,000 Jews scattered among half a million Arabs. The first *'aliya'* or immigration to Israel brought between 20 and 30,000 more Jews from Tsarist Russia between 1882 and 1903. Agricultural settlements were established at Rishon-le-Zion, Zikhron Yaakov, Rosh Pinnah, Petah Tikvah and elsewhere. Baron Edmond de Rothschild was responsible for financing nineteen more settlements, which took the total of the *Yishuv* pioneers to more than 5,000. In 1900 Rothschild's interests were taken over by the Jewish Colonisation Association led by Baron Maurice de Hirsh. Other Jewish bourgeois also invested in Palestine, particularly in grain production. It was a heterogeneous movement, with vague and contradictory ideologies and faced with enormous difficulties. It needed a theorist and an organiser.

Enter Herzl

Herzl, born in Budapest in 1860, was working as a journalist for the Viennese *Neue Freie Presse* when the Dreyfus affair blew up. He went to Paris to cover it for his paper. He was deeply shocked by the wave of anti-semitism which suddenly swept through France, which had been the first country in Europe to emancipate the Jews. His response was to publish a book in Vienna on 13 February 1896, *The Jewish State*, which argued that a Jewish state was the only solution to the Jewish 'problem'. He founded a weekly *Die Welt* the next year, which also saw the opening of the first world Zionist congress in Basle, under his chairmanship.

The 197 delegates adopted the Basle Programme which set out a very ambitious programme for the World Zionist Organisation. The aim of Zionism was declared to be 'to create for the Jewish people a home in Palestine secured by public law!' The Congress put forward the following means to achieve these aims:

'1. The promotion, on suitable lines, of the colonisation of Palestine by Jewish agricultural and industrial workers
2. The organisation and binding together of the whole of Jewry by means of appropriate institutions, local and international, in accordance with the laws of each country

3. The strengthening and fostering of Jewish national sentiment and consciousness
4. Preparatory steps towards obtaining government consent, where necessary, to the attainment of the aim of Zionism'.

With these as their aims Herzl and his supporters set out to win over their co-religionists and more especially to acquire the backing of powerful supporters for their cause. The founder of Zionism managed to obtain interviews with the Ottoman sultan Abdul Hamid, Kaiser Wilhelm II of Germany, the Pope, King Victor Emmanuel of Italy, the British prime minister Joseph Chamberlain, and even with the two Tsarist ministers Plehve and Witte who had been responsible for the terrible Russian pogroms in Poland. Argentina, Cyprus, the Belgian Congo, Mozambique, Sinai and Uganda were all suggested as possible sites for the Jewish homeland, but the Zionist Organisation – which really meant Russian and Polish Zionists – were adamant that it had to be Palestine.

Theodor Herzl died on 3 July 1904, without his dream having been realised. The day after the 1897 Congress in Basle he had written in his diary 'I have created the Jewish State in Basle. If I were to say that in public today the response would be laughter all round. The world will understand, maybe in 5 years, certainly in 50.' Israel declared its independence fifty years and nine months later.

After its founder's death the movement grew very slowly. But as congress followed congress the influence of the Zionist Organisation spread. The Jewish National Fund (Keren Kayemet) was set up to provide for the purchase of land. But there was considerable opposition – from Jews as well as other people. The opposition included orthodox Jews, for whom the state of Israel can only come into being as a result of the intervention of God, in the form of the Messiah; bourgeois liberals, who were commited to emancipation and assimilation, were also opposed to Zionism, as were the Marxists, who urged Jewish and non-Jewish workers in all countries to unite. It was by no means easy for the Zionists to win support.

The Jewish presence in Palestine, on the other hand,

was steadily growing. The second *aliyah*, mostly Russian in origin but socialist in perspective, brought in between 35,000 and 40,000 new immigrants from 1903 to 1914. Dozens of new colonies were set up: there were 47 by 1914. Jerusalem and Haifa grew larger. In 1909 the town of Tel Aviv sprang up out of the ground north of Jaffa. Hebrew, the literary and liturgical language, began to be used in daily life. The first 'oriental' Jews arrived in 1908 from the Yemen. They took the place of the Arab fellahs on the farms. The first kibbutz, Deganyah, was started in 1909. At the outbreak of the First World War the *yishuv* numbered some 80,000 people, 11,500 of whom were living in new settlements. But, to put this wave of new arrivals into perspective, it should be remembered that during the same period two or three million Jews left their homes not to go to Palestine but to go to Western Europe or to the Americas.

The Zionists' major achievement did not come for another three years: with the Balfour declaration their quest for a homeland at last acquired the official recognition that they had been seeking.

But why did Zionism acquire such influence at this time, and why was it to grow tenfold in the decades to come? A number of linked factors, which it is necessary to disentangle, came together to ensure its success.

The fundamental basis of Zionism was the misery of Jews in Central and Eastern Europe. In his book *Zionism against Israel* Nathan Weinstock justifiably argues that the movement was the product of the nineteenth century decomposition of the feudal structure of the Tsarist and Austro-Hungarian Empires coupled with the decadent phase of capitalism in western Europe. Thus the socio-economic basis of Jewish life in Eastern Europe was weakened and at the same time there was a halt in the process of proletarianisation and assimilation.

The exclusion of the Jews from capitalist society was accompanied by a ferocious upsurge in anti-semitism. Pogroms occurred in Eastern Europe in 1881, 1883, 1903 and 1905, while the West witnessed the Dreyfus affair. Jewish bitterness and feelings of disillusion were all the more strong given the moves towards emancipation which had seemed irreversible: starting with the French Revolutionary Law dated 28 September 1791, similar legislation had been passed throughout Europe ranging from the Netherlands in 1796 to the Ottoman Empire in 1908. The sole exceptions were Rumania and Russia – where emancipation followed the Bolshevik revolution in 1917. It is easy to understand the shocked reaction of Western Jews to this new wave of anti-semitism when we recall what Heinrich Graetz, the historian of the Jewish people, had written in 1870 describing the feeling of joy in the civilised world that the Jewish community had at long last achieved 'not only justice and liberty but also a degree of respect'.

But these motivating factors needed favourable conditions in the outside world to be fully effective. The imperial powers had long had their eyes on Palestine. By adding their weight to the burgeoning Zionist movement, the rival powers would be able to advance their own ambitions. Theodore Herzl was well aware of this and pointed out that the advantages of his proposals to each in turn, thereby attracting the label 'unscrupulous' from the historian Walter Laqueur. To the British he mentioned the protection of their lines of communication to Egypt; to the Russians he presented Zionism as a barrier to revolutionary infection; to the Germans he was able to offer the prospect of getting rid of a sector of their population that could not be assimilated; he promised the Sultan that if they were successful the Jews would pour money into his depleted coffers. The successors of the father of Zionism have certainly learnt from his approach to political matters! Zionism was a special phenomenon in a century full of nationalist movements. It came on the scene late, as a defence mechanism, while its romantic idealism soon gave way to colonial vested interests. The very foundations on which it was built were unstable.

Questionable Evidence

Zionism has four basic premises. Theodor Herzl deduced the inevitability of the Jews coming together in their own state from: the existence of a Jewish people; the

impossibility of their assimilation into any other country;
their historic rights over Palestine; the absence of any
other people there. However these are no more than
assertions. They are not proof.

'A European Jew goes off to look for his fellow Jews in
China. After much wandering he finally comes across a
synagogue in a back street in Shanghai. He goes in. The
Chinese Jews who are praying there are at first astonished,
and then become threatening. So he shouts out, "But I'm a
Jew too, just like you". They point to their slanting eyes
and tell him "You don't look like one". ' This old story
shows what any visit to Israel makes quite clear: the
so-called 'Jewish race' or 'Jewish blood', as it is sometimes
called, only exists as a figment of anti-semitic fantasy. In a
discussion about the definition of the term 'Jew', to which
we shall return later, Israeli supreme court judge Haim
Cohen let slip this heartfelt remark: 'It is bitterly ironical
that circumstances have led us to use the same biological
and racist theses put forward by the Nazis as the basis of
the official definition of Jewishness in the State of Israel'.

His remark caused such a scandal that he had to
withdraw it.

So, if there is no such thing as a racial definition, what
other criteria determine Jewishness? Religion? But a lot of
people who are said to be Jews are non-believers, or do not
believe any more. In any case the fact that many people
share the same faith does not necessarily mean that they
belong to a 'catholic people' or a 'buddhist people'. Where
they live? Even today only one fifth of Jews live in Israel,
the others have chosen to remain scattered throughout a
hundred different countries, submerged in an infinite
variety of different traditions, cultures and customs. How
about language? A large majority of Jews speak neither
Hebrew nor its derivatives, Judeo-German (yiddish),
Judeo-Spanish, (the spoken form, *Djudezmo*, the liturgical
form *Ladino*) or any of the forms of Judeo-Arabic. In fact
there is no single feature that all Jews have in common.
'You're a Jew if you think you're a Jew.' It certainly seems
that whether or not you feel you are Jewish is the most
useful way of looking at what Jewishness is. But what do
you feel? In countries like Poland or Russia where there

were large numbers of Jews with shared customs, homes and history plus of course language and religion, a feeling of identity was strengthened by successive persecutions. Zionism found most of its supporters in these areas. These 'national minorities' have almost completely disappeared, as a result of extermination by the Nazis, through massive emigration to Palestine or by a process of assimilation which left only the loosest form of community identity. More often than not this happened as result of a combination of all three elements. On the other hand, a real nation has come into being in Israel to which the majority of the world's Jews feel attached to some extent. The majority of the survivors of Nazi genocide, even those who were most fully assimilated into the countries where they lived, felt a resurgence of the myth of Israel as the only place left to go to. This is without doubt the basis of the very special relationship which Jews have with Israel. The Vatican and Mecca do not have the same significance for Catholics and Muslims.

Experience has shown that the contention that Jews cannot be assimilated into other societies is false, although it is true that the upsurge in antisemitism at the end of the nineteenth century slowed down the progress in emancipation. The holocaust had a lasting traumatic effect on Jewish consciousness. The emancipation process began again. As we have already seen the majority of Jews did not head for Israel, though a minority did. Elsewhere integration proceeded rapidly. Official Jewish and Zionist organisations only represented small, albeit active, minorities of the Jewish population. Once the language was forgotten and the religion no longer practised, the culture and traditions started to fade and all that remained was a rather vague feeling of 'Jewishness' which the policies of the government in Israel often did little to enhance.

'We have the right to be here,' said David Ben Gurion in 1936, a phrase which Golda Meir was to borrow from him 30 years later. 'The existence of this country is the fulfilment of a promise made by God himself: it would be ridiculous to ask God to justify its legitimacy'. The idea of the 'promised land' for the 'chosen people' stems from

Genesis, chapter 15, verse 18: 'On that day the Lord made a covenant with Abraham saying, Unto thy seed have I given this land from the river of Egypt unto the great river, the River Euphrates'.

With due respect to Golda Meir, in the eyes of the law, and even from a common sense point of view, no religious text can possibly bestow legitimacy on a people's claim to ownership of territory 3,500 years after the event. The Jews were not even the first people there. Furthermore no fewer than eleven other peoples have conquered and occupied Palestine in the course of history. As has often been pointed out the Jewish 'right' to Israel is based on an occupation which came to an end nineteen centuries ago. Absurd results would obviously ensue were these criteria to be applied worldwide.

We are told that, since it is the faith of the chosen people, the Jewish religion does not seek new converts. This is pure fiction. After their dispersion the Jews converted large numbers of people, from India to Gaul, from Rome to China, from Ethiopia to North Africa and from Asia Minor to Germany. There were even a few Jewish kingdoms in the wake of the conversion of a number of monarchs and their subjects, such as the Jewish state in Southern Arabia in the sixth century and the Jewish Khazar state in South-West Russia in the eighth century. In fact the Jewish diaspora consists of such a mixture of peoples that it is likely that Palestinian 'Arabs' have more of the ancient Hebrew in their make-up than do the diaspora Jews themselves.

'There is no such thing as the Palestinians'. This argument, which has been put forward by all the Zionists from Theodor Herzl to Itzhak Shamir, has been decisively refuted by the history of the struggle of the Palestinian people. When the first Russian colonists arrived in Palestine in 1882 there were 500,000 Arabs living there. People only tend to see what they want to. Although Herzl may have chosen to ignore the Palestinians, the Russian Zionist Asher Ginsberg, known as Ahad Haam, had these words of warning for his fellows on his return from a journey to the 'promised land'. 100 years later we are still struck by his lucidity: 'We tend to think of the Arabs as wild desert people who either don't see or don't understand what is going on around them. This is a big mistake. The Arabs, and particularly the city-dwellers, see and understand both what we are doing and what we would like to do in Palestine … If we ever get big enough to really start treading on their toes it will not be easy to get them out of our way'.

In the Shadow of London

Herzl wrote to Cecil Rhodes, one of the British 'conquerors' of Southern Africa, arguing that this was also a colonial project. As we have seen, Herzl went looking anywhere and everywhere for backers to help bring about the implementation of his programme. The people who succeeded him at the head of the Zionist Organisation concentrated their efforts on Great Britain, for reasons which have been explained in the first part of this book. To sum it up briefly, of all the great powers Britain occupied the best strategic position in the Middle East and was therefore best placed to facilitate Zionism's progress. It was also in Britain's interests that Zionism should succeed. Chaim Weizmann, the main Zionist leader between the wars admitted that they wanted to be a British protectorate. And he argued that a Jewish Palestine would be in Britain's interests, particularly in relation to the Suez Canal.

His judgement proved to be accurate. The 1917 Balfour declaration, followed by the League of Nations mandate in 1922, conferred international legitimacy on the idea of a 'Jewish National Homeland'. Everything came together to ensure the successful development of the Zionist cause. Having once got British backing, the Zionist leaders were to manipulate their backers right up until the start of the Second World War, yet never failing to grasp opportunities to play the great powers off against each other. They did it subtly, exerting the heaviest pressure possible on the British while consistently presenting their actions as being in British interests. They concealed their long-term aim. In contrast to the Palestinians they were quite happy to make all sorts of compromises to further their cause.

The British politicians, however, were not all taken in. Men such as Edwin Montagu and Lord Curzon opposed the notion of a Jewish National Homeland. Lord Curzon in particular argued that behind the stated aim of a national homeland lay the aim of the Zionists to establish a Jewish state with authority over the Arabs living in Palestine. However what mattered for the British was maintaining their presence in Palestine. These interests were admirably served by Jewish colonisation.

The British government had another problem: the need not to incur Arab hostility. Successive Palestinian risings against Jewish immigration were met with gestures of appeasement in London. After all the Balfour declaration pledged that 'nothing shall be done which may prejudice the civil and religious rights of existing non-Jewish communities in Palestine'. White papers in 1922 and 1930 provided the British with some room for manoeuvre in their support for the Zionist cause. It took the great revolt of 1936 to force the mandatory power to change its position: the 1939 white paper drastically limited immigration and land purchase. Britain, though pushed into pro-Arab policies by the oncoming war, could do so in the knowledge that at least in the short-term the Zionists had no other ally to turn to.

A 'revisionist' Zionist tendency, personified by Vladimir Zeev Jabotinsky, arose in opposition to the pro-British strategy symbolised by Chaim Weizmann. Jabotinsky, a Russian writer and journalist, had some curious friends. Between 1919 and 1921 in Russia he had sought to form an alliance with the counter-revolutionary general Petlioura, who was well known to Jews for the pogroms perpetrated by his troops. Jabotinsky dreamed of an anti-soviet Jewish army unit. It was an obsession with him: he was responsible for the *Yishuv*'s first 'Jewish legion'. A dyed-in-the-wool militarist, Jabotinsky openly admired Mussolini and the fascists.

But the split between the Zionist majority and the revisionists was over more than personalities: it was over the aims of the Jewish people and the best means of achieving them. While Weizmann was prepared to water down his programme Jabotinsky made no bones at all about his aims: 'The aim of the Zionist movement is to create a Jewish state ... territory on both sides of the River Jordon ... hence today's watchword: a new political campaign and the militarisation of Jewish youth in Eretz Israel and the diaspora'. From this quasi-fascist standpoint Jabotinsky poured scorn on what he called the 'humility' of the Zionist movement's relations with Great Britain. This strategic, ideological and tactical struggle has been waged throughout Zionist history, from the *Yishuv* to present-day Israel.

The struggle was particularly ferocious between the wars. In 1925 Jabotinsky had acquired a party, the Tsohar, a youth movement, the Betar, and a militia, the Irgun. He now attacked the socialist majority which at the time controlled the *Yishuv* and the Zionist movement. The revisionists left the World Zionist Organisation in 1935 and set up their own body. The split took place in all the *Yishuv's* organisations, including its trade union, the Histadrut. Their ferocious anti-Arab terrorism and extreme anti-communist and anti-socialist violence, coupled wth extravagant praise of fascism, was so shocking that David Ben Gurion nicknamed their leader 'Vladimir Hitler'.

During the war, when the Zionist movement allied itself with Britain against the Axis powers, a revisionist splinter group even went so far as to propose an alliance with Nazi Germany. Although the Reich did not follow up these initiatives, the Lehy nevertheless embarked on anti-British terrorism in 1943, followed a year later by the Irgun, now under the leadership of Menachem Begin, following Jabotinsky's death in 1940. This marked the beginning of a wave of attacks which became so widespread, as we have seen, that they led to British withdrawal from Palestine.

The Herut (Freedom) Party, founded by Menachem Begin in 1948, saw itself as part of the revisionist tradition. The new leader of the far right was true to both the aims and the methods of his master: he claimed both sides of the Jordan for Israel. Both his discourse and his actions were akin to fascism. It is said that David Ben Gurion, seeing in him 'a real Hitlerite', refused to his dying day to mention his name. In tracing the development of the state of Israel we also plot the irresistible rise of an extremist who came to power twenty-nine years after independence.

Though it grew thanks to Britain, the *Yishuv* became the state of Israel thanks to the United States. The same strategy which led the Zionist leadership to formulate their demand for a 'Jewish state' in the 'Biltmore Programme' of 1942 also led them to take another look at their alliance policy. During the First World War Britain had rightly seemed the best 'protector' available. The growth of United States power during the Second World War made it clear that American support would be vital to achieve the transformation of Zionism into statehood. From this period onwards, the United States, which was now the dominant world power, became the central focus of Israel's international policy.

People and Land

Let us go back to 1918. The old Jewish communities and the first two *aliyot* only took the total number of Jews in Palestine to 60,000: less than 10% of the population. Immigration started again in the wake of the Balfour declaration and carried on until 1939. But there was not a steady flow, as the chart shows.

The movement of Jewish people into Palestine can be seen in two distinct phases: before and after Hitler's seizure of power. Between 1919 and 1931 there were only 116,796 new arrivals – an average of 8,343 per year. And from this figure we must deduct those who left as a consequence of the post-1925 economic crisis in the *Yishuv* and the second *aliya* which had had the same problems. So, at the end of 1931 the total number of Jews in the 'Holy Land' only amounted to 175,000, 17.7% of the population. Between 1932 and 1939 247,723 new immigrants came, averaging 30,965 each year. This wave was different from those preceding it in two ways. Firstly in terms of motivation: they did not come because they were convinced Zionists but because they were fleeing Nazi threats. Secondly, they were different socially: most were middle class and came in greater numbers after the 1933 agreement between the Zionist Organisation and Berlin

Jewish immigration to Palestine and Israel

Date		Number	Main country of origin	Type of settler
1. Ottoman period				
1882-1903	1st Aliyah	20-30,000	Russia	'Lovers of Zion' and the 'Bilu' movement
1904-14	2nd Aliyah	35-40,000	Russia	Workers and pioneer socialists
2. British Mandate				
1919-23	3rd Aliyah	35,000	USSR, Poland, Baltic countries	Workers and pioneer socialists
1924-31	4th Aliyah	82,000	USSR, Poland, Balkans, Middle East	Middle classes
1932-38	5th Aliyah	217,000	Poland, Germany, Austria	Liberal professions, bourgeoisie
1939-48	6th Aliyah	153,000	Central and Eastern Europe, Balkans	People escaping Hitler's persecution, often clandestinely
3. Israel				*Percentage coming from Africa and Asia*
1948-51		690,000	Central and Eastern Europe, Yemen, Iraq, North Africa	50%
1952-54		55,000	North Africa, Rumania	76%
1955-57		165,000	North Africa, Egypt, Poland, Hungary	68%
1958-60		75,000	Rumania, Tunisia	36%
1961-64		230,000	Morocco	60%
1965-68		82,000	North Africa, Eastern Europe, Latin America	54%
1969-71		115,000	Eastern Europe, USA, Latin America	54%
1972-74		143,000	USSR	11%
1975-83		150,000	USSR	10%

permitting German Jews to export capital. To put things in perspective again: only 8.5% of the Jews leaving Germany and the occupied countries – 2,560,000 between 1935 and 1943 – went to Palestine. Nevertheless there were 429,605 Jews in 'Eretz Israel' in 1939: 28% of the total population. Despite the British blockade, a further 118,338, an average of 13,922 each year, joined them between the end of 1939 and independence – 14 May 1948. So the British mandate saw the proportion of Jews in Palestine rise from 10% to 30%

The first pioneers and their leaders were guided by the idea of 'the regeneration of the Jewish people through work'. The social structure of Jewish communities had been distorted for centuries by bans on Jews doing certain kinds of work. Manual work being generally forbidden, Jews engaged themselves predominantly in crafts, business, the professions of intellectual work. The socialist Zionists were determined to reverse this tendency. This was the ideology which motivated Jewish acquisition of Arab land. In 1897 the *Yishuv* had 204,000 dunams under cultivation. (A dunam is about a quarter of an acre.) In 1947 this figure had risen to 1,802,300 dunams. The number of colonies had gone up from 27 to over 300. Authorisation of this 'transfer' of land came from the Ottoman agricultural law which still applied. The land did not in fact belong to the farmers, but to rich absentee landlords who were often foreigners. They were responsible for the sale of 73% of the land bought by the Keren Kayemet (Jewish National Fund) and the P.J.C.A. (Palestine Jewish Colonisation Association), the former a public body, the latter in private hands. Once the courts had expelled the Arab families living there the land was symbolically rented out to Jewish farmers, but remained 'the inalienable property' of the Hebrew people, and could never be sold or let to Arabs.

The special nature of Jewish agricultural colonisation was also determined by the fact that the farms were collectives: co-operative *moshavim* and collective kibbutzim. More than half the land was farmed in this manner in 1947. The other half was in the hands of private owners who were quite happy to use Arab labour. In the co-operative and collective sectors the 'conquest of land' went hand in glove with the 'conquest of work', the so-called 'Hebrew work' campaign. The Zionists launched an all-out attack on Arab jobs. The idealistic pretext of not exploiting the Arabs concealed the real aim of the *Yishuv* leadership: to deprive the Palestinians not just of land but also of the means of subsistence. This campaign went on in the towns as well, aimed at workshops, businesses and shops which still had Arab employees. Posters went up saying 'Don't buy Arab goods' and 'Buy Hebrew'.

Urbanisation was speeding up as well as agricultural developments. The new city of Tel Aviv trebled in population between 1923 and 1926. The arrival of very large numbers of workers, engineers, technicians and, as we have seen, capitalists gave a great boost to Jewish industry despite the economic crisis. The Zionist leader Arlosoroff who was murdered in 1933, probably by the Revisionists, described these hordes of shop-keepers, artisans and small-time traders as the proletariat of the petty bourgeoisie. There were co-operative businesses in the urban sector of the economy, but to a lesser extent than in the countryside. The *Yishuv* ultimately included 2,200 co-operatives involved in all sectors of the economy, from industry to banking and insurance, transport and commerce. The biggest was the Tnuva which was responsible for the distribution of Jewish farm produce.

Contrary to the claims made by Zionist propaganda, Palestine did not look like a desert prior to 1882. It is true, though, that Jewish immigrants transformed it. Land was cleared, marshes drained and hills replanted with trees. Towns and factories sprang up like mushrooms. The road network was extended. A few figures bear witness to the growth in agricultural output: although cereal production remained more or less static at about 100,000 tonnes, citrus fruits rocked from 1.3 million crates in 1913 to 15 million in 1939, which accounted for 74% of *Yishuv* exports. Vegetable output went up 18-fold between 1922 and 1945. The financial, material and technical advantages at the disposal of the Jewish farming community were such that in 1944-45 they produced 28.3% of total agricultural output – excluding citrus fruit – from just 7.7% of the land. The industrial boom was equally remarkable. Taking the 1920-22 figures as 100, industrial production had reached 2,368 by 1937-38, and doubled again between 1939 and 1945. In 1926 Palestine produced 2.34 million kilowatts of electricity: in 1943 161.62 million.

The previous year's census noted 1907 Jewish firms employing 37,773 people, and 1,558 Arab firms employing 8,804 people. But if we add up the people employed in industry, services and agriculture, together with those working in the British military bases, the total now becomes 70,000 Jews and 90,000 Arabs.

The *Yishuv*'s overseas trade was already in deficit! In 1924 imports came to 5.27 million Palestinian pounds, exports amounted to 1.2 million. The gap was narrowed but not bridged. In 1945 £20m worth of exports were matched by imports of £40m. Export revenue had increased from 22% to 50% of import costs. The balance of payments was held steady by injections of Jewish capital from abroad, notably from the United States.

Obviously economic growth did not benefit everyone equally. Zionists like to boast about what this growth did for the Palestinians. There is no doubt that the standard of living, education and life expectancy of the Palestinian Arabs has increased faster than in neighbouring countries. What the 'benefactors' neglect to mention is the widening gulf between Jews and Arabs in Palestine. It takes many forms: in social terms the percentage of Arabs working in agriculture is three times higher than that of Jews; in industry it is the exact opposite; in terms of purchasing power the average annual income of a Jew is double that of an Arab; in consumer terms Jews spend 2.1 times more than Arabs on food, 4.3 times more on clothes, 3.7 times more on other consumer goods, 5.6 times more on housing, and so on. These statistics would need to be analysed further to ascertain whether they reflect the full impact of the threefold Jewish take-over of land, work and trade. The poverty and unemployment that resulted for large numbers of Arabs was one of the main causes of a succession of outbreaks of violence against Zionist immigration.

Birth of a Nation

Palestine was a small, sparsely populated, underdeveloped country. It was gradually transformed as a result of the massive influx of people coming to join the Jewish community, which made up a third of the population and occupied key positions in agricultural and industrial development. A Palestinian Jewish nation was growing up alongside the Palestinian Arab nation. The political and institutional organisation of the *Yishuv* contributed greatly to this.

Under the provisions of the mandate, the country was governed by a British civilian administration, with a high commissioner who had both legislative and executive powers. The assembly promised by the mandate was never elected: first the Arabs and then the Jews turned it down, the Jewish rejection being based on the Zionist Organisation's refusal to countenance 'anything that would ... (tend to) ... put the future of the country into the hands of the present majority population'. Thus the mandatory authority governed by decree, although recognising the relative autonomy of the judicial system, which was partly based on Ottoman and British civil tribunals, and partly on Jewish, Christian and Islamic religious courts.

Article 4 of the mandate stipulated that 'an appropriate Jewish agency shall be recognized as a public body for the purpose of advising and co-operating with the Administration of Palestine on such matters as the interests of the Jewish population in Palestine'. The first such Jewish agency – indeed it was specifically designated in the same League of Nations text – was to be the World Zionist Organisation, or to be exact its executive committee which was elected every other year by the congress. A suitably competent body, including prominent non-Zionist Jews was set up in 1929 under the auspices of the Zionist Organisation. It was called the Palestine Jewish Agency and was responsible for the foreign distribution of the immigration certificates issued by the British administration. It soon acquired a major political role. Through the Keren Kayemet it masterminded colonisation. It set up its own executive committee in Jerusalem chaired by the President of the Zionist Organisation. It had a special relationship with the mandate authorities and worked closely with them in all matters.

The *Yishuv* also delegated power to an assembly which was elected in 1920, 1925, 1931 and 1944 on the basis of proportional representation. The Vaad Leumi (National Council), which stemmed from the assembly was also seen as the guardian of Palestinian Jewish sovereignty. The roles of the Vaad Leumi and the Jewish Agency gradually became distinct. The former took care of things like education, health and social welfare, and the latter was in charge of immigration, land acquisition, security and 'foreign policy'.

Zionist political parties took root in Palestine. Most of them had their origins in the first *aliya*. The 'Left' was dominated by the Mapai (the initials of the Eretz Israel Labour Party). It grew out of the union of two socialist groups in November 1930: the Marxist Ahdut Ha-Avodah (United Workers) and the anti-Marxist Ha-Poele Ha-Zair (Young Workers). Under David Ben Gurion's leadership the Mapai was a reformist party, supporting alliance with right-wing Zionists and with Great Britain. Two left-wing organisations did not join the 1930 union. The Ha-Shomer Ha-Zair (The Young Watchmen) was very influential in the main kibbutzim federation, and advocated a binational state, as did the Poale Zion Smol (Left-wing Workers of Zion) which also sought membership of the Comintern, though without success. These two groups were the forerunners of the present-day Mapam. None of the groups that made up the Left questioned the fundamentals of Zionism. Socialist influence was mainly exerted through the Histadrut (the General Confederation of Jewish Workers) which was founded in 1920. It was not simply a trade union organisation. The Histadrut was also an employer – it owned many industrial businesses; a financier – it owned the Workers Bank; – an educational organisation running a tightly knit network of educational establishments; and a kind of social welfare body through the Kupat Holim (Health Insurance Fund).

The socialist parties' share of the vote in assembly elections came to 37% in 1920, 36.5% in 1925, 42.3% in 1931 and 59.1% in 1944. The right-wing Zionist leadership did not ignore this steady progress. The socialist Arlosoroff, whose name we have already mentioned, became Head of the Political Department of the Jewish Agency in 1931. Three other future socialist leaders joined the Zionist Organisation Executive in the same year: Ben Gurion, future Prime Minister of Israel, Moshe Shertok, future Foreign Minister and Prime Minister under the name of Sharett, and Eliezer Kaplan. One of them, David Ben Gurion, was appointed to head the executive of the Jewish Agency in 1935.

As control was gradually wrested from their grasp, the right split into two tendencies. The first Zionist Orgnisation was the General Zionists, which, as the voice of the Jewish bourgeoisie and property owners, had done very well out of the first *aliya* period from 1924 to 1931, which came to be known as the bourgeois *aliya*. Two wings vied with each other for leadership of the party: the moderates or 'A' group were in favour of coming to terms with the socialists and Great Britain; the others, the 'B' group, rejected this approach. The General Zionists obtained 19.7% of the votes in 1920, reached a highpoint in 1925 with 35.8%, fell back badly to 9.9% in 1931 and went up again to 20.5% in 1944. Their poor score in 1931 was because of competition from the revisionists. The Revisionist Party, while posing as the defender of the bosses' rights and supporting strike-breakers, imitated the Fascist Leagues during the economic crisis by making political capital out of middle class fears. On the only two occasions it put up candidates, in 1925 and 1931, its vote was 6.3% and then 22.5%.

The religious parties were also made up of two factions, distinguished by whether or not they were part of the *Yishuv*. The first group included the Mizrahi (Orientals) and its labour wing Poale Ha-Mizrahi. They hoped to bring about the union of religious traditions and Zionist ideals in a national-religious Judaism. This was strongly opposed by the Agudat Israel Party and its 'worker' splinter group Poale Agudat Israel, who denied the legitimacy of the Zionists and the parallel state they had set up. The first and only occasion on which all the religious parties took part in elections was in 1920. They totalled 20.3% of the votes. In subsequent elections only the Mizrahi and the Poale Ha-Mizrahi sought the voters' support, obtaining 8.8% in 1925, 7% in 1931 and 16.6% in 1944.

Another non-Zionist party, albeit a very small one, set about a very difficult task: that of bringing Jewish and Arab workers together. For its pains it met with repression from the British, and hostility from the Zionists and Palestinian reactionaries. The Communist Party of Palestine had been founded by left-wing Russian Jews in 1922, but was weakened by internal splits caused by ideological differences and the problems of being Jewish anti-Zionists. It took Comintern pressure in the 30s to push the party into recruiting Arab members. The Comintern's changes of direction also had their effect. When news of the 1929 riots came out Moscow directed the communists to support the Palestinian nationalists, but this soon degenerated into mere acceptance of the line taken by its 'feudal' leadership. Tension between Arabs and Jews reached such a high level that the party split in two in 1943, the Arabs forming the National Liberation League and the Jews the Communist Party of Palestine. Soviet support for the proposed partition of Palestine caused more trouble. Arab and Jewish communists joined forces again to found the Maki (Communist Party of Israel) on 22 October 1948. The creation of the Communist Party of Jordan in 1951 was the work of communists in the West Bank.

Some small Zionist groups also declared themselves favourably disposed towards a binational state and advocated friendship between Arabs and Jews. Other than the ones we have mentioned – the Ha-Shomer Ha-Zair and the Poale Zion Smol – this was also the stance taken by the Brit Shalom (Peace Alliance) and the Ihud (Union) Group. The Reformed Synagogue Rabbi Judah Magnes came from this last group. But they did not flourish within the Zionist Movement.

The *Yishuv* had its own language which was modernised and popularised thanks to Eliezer Ben Yehuda: 75% of the Jews in the country used it by 1948. The whole range of public services, from health to education, was available. An embryonic army existed in the shape of the Haganah and Palmakh groups, plus the Irgun terrorists. There was nothing missing that could hinder the *Yishuv* from transforming itself from a religious community into a nation and then on to a state. On 14 May 1948 the independence of Israel was proclaimed.

1948 Onwards

From 1948 to 1987, the birth and development of the Jewish state have always been accompanied by a background of war. Its history is littered with wars: the War of Independence from 1948-9, the Suez Expedition in 1956, the Six Day War in 1967, Yom Kippur in 1973 and the invasion of Lebanon in 1982. We spent a long time in the first chapter looking at the endless conflicts between Israel and her neighbours. Here we must draw attention to the main changes which have occurred within Israel itself.

To start with there is a demographic change: the population of Israel has gone up from 650,000 in 1948 to nearly 3,400,000 in 1983 – 5.23 times greater. This enormous increase is primarily the result of immigration as shown in the table on page 65. The first phase, from 1948 to the end of 1951 brought 750,000 Jews who had escaped death in the camps, had been evacuated from Eastern Europe, or had come to the 'promised land' from Arab countries. This flood of new arrivals dried up, but started again in 1954. The struggle for independence in Morocco and Tunisia, followed by the Algerian war prompted many Jewish settlers in North Africa to leave their homes. The majority went to France but a good number chose to go to Israel. The Suez affair and the Six Day War gave rise to antisemitic feelings in Arab countries and led many Jews to turn to Tel Aviv. Between 1954 and 1971 an average of 50,000 – 60,000 immigrants a year arrived, mostly from the Third World. 1972 saw a new phenomenon with the departure of 260,000 Jews from the Soviet Union, but although they had visas to go to Israel, the majority opted instead for the United States and Western Europe. This flow of population slowed quite considerably with the ending of detente between East and West. In passing let us note that the growth in the Jewish population of Israel slowed down each decade: 4.7% from 1950-60, 3.1% from 1960-70, 2.6% from 1970-76 and 1.9% from 1976-81.

The third chapter of this book is about the fate of the Arabs. At this point we only need to mention that after the enforced exodus of 1947-49 there were only 160,000 Arabs in Israel, 13.6% of the total population 35 years later there are more than 700,000 or 17.5% of the total. Since Israel has chosen to ignore U.N. resolutions calling for the return of refugees, the only explanation for this increase is a high birth-rate.

The Israeli economy grew even faster than the population. Between 1950 and 1981 gross national product went up 10.6 times, *per capita* production 3.39 times. Average annual growth in agricultural output was close to 7%. Taking the 1949 industrial output figures as 100, by 1981 output had risen to 688. A highly skilled workforce, and injections of foreign capital, made up for Israel's poor natural resources, particularly its lack of raw materials, energy and water. Growth was not uninterrupted. It was inevitable that the creation of the new state and a sudden twofold increase in population would cause problems, but after these diffficulties were resolved the next fifteen years, from 1950 to 1965, were euphoric. The 1966-67 economic crisis was overcome thanks to the Six Day War. New defence requirements in the electronic, aeronautical and armament fields, and the new markets in the Gaza Strip and on the West Bank where cheap labour was also available, helped to get the economy moving again. But the economy did not recover from the Yom Kippur war and the oil price shocks which followed. Economic growth, like population growth, slowed down as time passed: 5.2% from 1950-60, 4.9% from 1960-70, 3% from 1970-76 and 1% from 1976-81.

Inextricably linked to these changes was a profound transformation in the nature of society. The distribution of the workforce changed. The number of people employed in agriculture went down from 18% in 1949 to 6.1% in 1981; in the manufacturing sector the figure remained more or less stable at around 30%, while the service sector climbed from 52% to 63.2%. It should be noted however that tens of thousands of manual workers from the occupied territories are not included in these statistics. The standard of living went up and, though not

up to western levels, *per capita* consumption more than
trebled in thirty years. A kind of 'cultural revolution'
occurred, aspects of which Nicola Garriba describes in his
book *Lo Stato di Israele*. 13 million books are printed in
Israel and 3.5 million theatre tickets sold every year. The
three principal classical orchestras give 180 concerts each
year and attract more than 40,000 subscribers. There are
750 public libraries, used by 21% of Israelis. 11 out of
every 1,000 people are involved in research, which
accounts for 1.4% of G.N.P. In 1982 1,200,000 people
attended schools of all kinds. The 1948 figure was
138,000.

Bearing in mind that the population of Israel is only
4,000,000 these figures are even more surprising. But
what happens to the fruits of these achievements? The
developments we have just outlined have been
accompanied by a three-way split in Israeli society:

– between Jews and Arabs: Only the crumbs of these
achievements have fallen to the Israeli Arabs. The Arabs
in the occupied territories have had next to nothing.

– between rich and poor Jews: in 1983 500,000 families
were living below the poverty line, three times more than
in 1977.

– between European and American Jews and 'Oriental'
Jews. Class divisions tend to correspond quite closely to
those between the communities, as we shall see. But the
really glaring paradox is that Israeli independence has
actually served to increase its dependence. Deficit is
endemic to the economy; and its causes are legion. Jewish
immigration is expensive: $3,000 per head according to
Israeli figures. More than anything else war has gobbled
up the state's resources: on average defence accounts for
30% of G.N.P. The occupation of Gaza and the West Bank
has cost even more. In 1983 settlementss cost a billion
dollars. Although exports covered 67.8% of imports in
1981 as against 11.7% in 1950 the overall commercial
deficit is still very, very high. Indeed it is so high that Israel
is now one of the most heavily indebted countries in the
world: $24 billion at the end of 1983, or $6,000 per head.
Poland and Brazil, the two countries most often
mentioned in this context, owe $7,200 per head.

So without foreign aid Israel would have been bankrupt long ago. Even the huge contributions from Jewish communities abroad and especially from the United States would not have been enough to stave off insolvency. The Jewish state rightly received war damages from West Germany amounting to $770 million between 1952 and 1965, quite apart from individual damages awarded to Nazi victims. But the United States has been chiefly responsible for keeping Israel afloat. Between 1948 and 1983 the United States government paid out $40-50 million in one form or another to the Tel Aviv government. American 'aid' to its 'strategic ally' reached such proportions in 1983 that it came to $900 per head, not counting individual contributions from American Jews. In contrast the average annual income in Egypt was just under $660 per head.

Democracy Under Threat

Propaganda can be misleading. Zionists like to paint a picture of Israel as a democratic paradise surrounded by a totalitarian Arab hell. It quite shamelessly passes over the cancer stemming from wars and occupations which today is gnawing away at the state of Israel and threatening the very heart of Israeli liberties. The most obvious symptoms of this malaise are the events at the Sabra and Shatila refugee camps, the Gush Emunim and Rabbi Kahane fascist groups, the diktats from extremist religious groups and even the appointment of ex-terrorists to the office of prime minister. But even when these factors are taken into account the Arab description of Israel as a fascist dictatorship is not acceptable. It overlooks one element which is quite clear: the Israeli state has a western-style parliamentary democracy. What is more it is the only one in the area.

In Israel legislative power is exercised by the Knesset, a single chamber elected every four years by universal suffrage in a secret ballot using a nationwide proportional representation system. All citizens, Jews and Arabs alike, can vote at 18 and stand for election at 21. The 120 members of parliament make laws, determine the budget and control the executive. The government, which is subject to a vote of confidence, can be censured; when called upon to respond to parliament it must do so within 21 days. The Knesset can only be dissolved by itself, at which point a general election has to take place.

Executive power is held solely by the government. Power is vested in the government by the Knesset, to whom it is answerable. The government, comprising the prime minister and ministers, each of whom has a deputy, is legally obliged to adhere to 'coalition discipline' as are all members of parliamentary groups. According to the constitution the government is empowered on behalf of the state to take whatever action it chooses on condition that the action proposed does not come under the authority of another body. This shows just how widespread are the powers of the prime minister and his or her colleagues. In the field of foreign affairs they can go so far as to ratify treaties. It is interesting to note in passing that nowhere is there any mention of the way in which decisions relating to war and peace are taken. In the event of the resignation of the government, the death of the prime minister, or a vote of no confidence, the government must continue to carry out its duties until a new one takes over, during which time ministers can neither resign nor be co-opted.

The President of the state is elected by an absolute majority of the Knesset for a period of five years, renewable only once. With the exception of choosing the prime minister the president's functions are purely honorary and subject to government confirmation. The president has the power to grant clemency, after agreement with the minister of justice. The death penalty is only invoked in Israel for treason in times of war and for Nazi war crimes: it has only once been carried out, in the case of Adolf Eichmann. The only president to have given the presidency a more active political role was Itzhak Navon, an open-minded Sephardic Labour Party member, between 1978 and 1983.

The independence of Israeli justice is strengthened by its complexity. Over and above Ottoman law which has now become more or less obsolete, the legal system is divided into three parts. Personal law (marriage, divorce and wills, subject to the agreement of the beneficiaries) is handled by different religious courts. The legal system dating from the time of the British mandate is still in operation. An Israeli system comprising civil and military courts has been set up at all levels right up to the supreme court. This court has some degree of autonomy, and has on occasion upheld complaints such as that lodged by the Palestinians against the Israeli military administration. The same applies to commissions of enquiry such as those presided over by Judge Agranat into negligence during the war of Yom Kippur and by Judge Kahane into the Sabra and Shatila affair, which both caused considerable public concern.

Political parties are a major feature of Israeli democracy. The exceptional richness of political life is explained by a number of factors: the history of the *Yishuv*, the strong ideological motivation of the people who built the state of Israel, and the present system of proportional representation. Political analysts illustrate this by pointing to the high level of electoral participation – in the region of 80%, despite the fact that many citizens live abroad – and to the high number of organisations standing for election. Each time the voters are consulted some 20 or 30 parties vie with each other for votes.

Since 1948, as indeed before that time, three large blocs have predominated:

– the workers' bloc, now called the Maarakh, (Labour Front), including the Labour Party and the Mapam.

– the right-wing bloc, known today as the Likud (Union) mainly comprised of the Herut (Freedom) Party which came out of the Revisionist movement and the liberal party originating from the Zionists.

– lastly, the religious bloc, whose various components we shall look at later on.

Outside of these coalitions, or situated on their fringes, a number of other parties operate: on the left the Rakah (New Communist List, Communist Party of Israel), the zionist-pacifist Shelli (National Israeli Left), as well as other pacifist groups which we shall look at later; on the far right the Tehia (Renaissance) and the Gush Emunim

(Bloc of the Faith) which overlap with the Likud. A number of features of these parties stem from the electoral system and their organisation into coalitions: the executive committees draw up the lists of party candidates, negotiate coalitions when in power, and impose rigorous voting discipline. As a result party leaders retain power with quite remarkable continuity. Nathan Yathan, in a study of leaders re-elected at party congresses, draws attention to the following figures: 65.3% of the Labour Party, 60.2% of the National Religious Party and 71.5% of the Herut Party leaders are re-elected by congress. Since 1973 parties have been funded out of public funds in proportion to the number of seats they have in the Knesset, and their finances closely scrutinised. Through its branches, and also through the significant sector of the economy which it controls, the Trade Union Federation Histadrut acts as an important and well-run lobby. Nor should the press be overlooked: it is one of the most widely-read in the world, with 27 dailies, 14 of which are in Hebrew. The five largest sell 650,000 copies per day, which works out at one for every 6.2 people in the country. In comparison, in France the 5 largest newspapers sell 2,300,000 per day, which works out at one for every 23.5 people.

However this political life, which at first sight seems so democratic, has been undermined by the conflict between Israel, its Arab neighbours and the Palestinians, which has now been going for 38 years. Marxist tradition holds that 'any nation that oppresses another forges its own chains'. The people of Israel are living proof of this. Wars, the chauvinistic nationalism which has come from them, the occupation of Arab territories and the oppression of the people living there, have brought about the degeneration of Israeli society. On the economic front the defence budget has been a constant drain on the nation. The repeated blood-lettings have driven the majority of the population to the limits of their endurance. The terrible tide of poverty has divided society on ethnic lines between the Western Jews, who tend to be better off, and the Oriental Jews, who tend to be near the bottom of the social scale. On the political level dissatisfaction and chauvinism have swung the pendulum to the right for the first time in Israeli history. Worse still, the values and operation of Israeli democracy itself have been shaken to their foundations.

Before looking at each of these aspects in turn we must ask ourselves what has happened to the ideals of the *Yishuv* pioneer socialists, as Israel witnesses in amazement an Oriental Jew murdered by a Western Jew, or a Pacifist Jew assassinated by an Extremist Jew. Or as fascist groups spread right across society reaching right into the heart of the state. At the same time Jewish colonists operate outside the law with impunity. Time and again the reality of torture and brutality is revealed. And there is more. The real sword of Damocles hanging over everything is the state of emergency which was declared in 1948 and has never been lifted. The legislation relating to it is worrying on two counts. Firstly the Defence Regulations (Emergency), introduced in 1945 under the British mandate, empower the government to take absolutely any form of action. These are still in operation. Under their provisions associations can be dissolved, people can be banished, put under house arrest or in preventive detention, special courts can be set up, and so on. Another weapon was added to this arsenal by a Special Ordinance in 1948, of which Article 9 reads 'Once the Knesset has decreed a state of emergency the government can empower the prime minister or a minister to take all steps necessary to ensure the defence of the state, public safety and the maintenance of indispensable public services'. Although initially used against Israeli Arabs and the Palestinians in the occupied territories, these exceptional measures have now become ordinary, everyday tools in the hands of the state, on a permanent basis. There is a parallel here between the Israeli experience and that undergone in France at the time of the colonial wars: in the long run the methods which a government uses to subdue its colonies are used against the population at home.

There is one other surprising feature of the Israeli state: although it has a declaration of independence and laws have been passed from time to time for the purpose of organising state affairs, Israel still does not have a

constitution. David Ben Gurion's argument, put forward
in 1949, in favour of putting off drawing up a constitution
– largely on the grounds that they should wait until large
numbers of Jews had arrived in Israel – only partially
covered up a political issue: unwillingness to face up to the
problems posed by the religious interests. The problem
over the constitution was due to one of the fundamental
and crucial contradictions of the Jewish state: the position
and status of religion.

Secular or Theocratic?

In *The Jewish State*, Herzl argued against any notion that
Israel would become theocratic. History has not treated
these illusions of his kindly. After a long period of
evolution Israel certainly looks like a theocratic state, if we
understand a theocracy as a state in which religion and
religious leaders play a very prominent role.

As we saw when examining the basic theses of Zionism,
it all goes back to the definition of 'the Jewish people'. For
religious Jews it is essentially to do with the laws of the
Torah. There is only one law, God's law, which is made up
of the written law, the Torah, and the oral law which
comes from the Talmud. This law does not just govern
Moses' people's religious observance, it relates to every
important part of life: food, work and rest, holidays,
marriage and divorce, sex, funerals, and so on. Regardless
of whether or not the religious leaders have come to terms
with Zionism or recognised the state of Israel, since 1948
they have concentrated their efforts in pursuit of one
objective: to make their law the law of the state of Israel, to
impose it on everyone, believers and unbelievers alike, and
in so doing acquire positions of power for themselves.

Even in the days of the *Yishuv* religious groups were a
real political force. As now there were two groups. On the
Zionist wing the key role was held by the Mafdal or
National Religious Party which stemmed from the
Mizrahi. In any election it is assured of winning about 10
of the 120 seats, its highest score being 16 in 1949, and its
lowest 6 in 1981. In 81 many of its voters turned to the
Likud, the far Right, or to a new Sephardi splinter group,

the Tami, which won 3 seats. The non-Zionist wing is
composed of the Agudat Israel and Poale Agudat Israel
parties which on average win 4 to 6 seats in each election.
The combined strength of the religious parties varies
between 13 and 18, but they represent a moral, political
and numerical force without which it is impossible to form
a durable coalition. From 1949 to 1974 the Mafdal was
allied to the Labour Party, and had members in every
government except briefly in 1958 and 1974. In
government it monopolised not just the religious affairs
ministry but also the vital post of minister of the interior,
together with other posts. They were pushed out of the
Rabin government in December 1976; and with one eye on
the forthcoming 1977 elections, they joined up with the
Likud. They have been in government with them ever
since. Since no government can survive without it the
National Religious Party has been able to impose stringent
conditions as the price of its support.

The fact that the Jewish state has no constitution is
because neither of the apparently secular parties has
argued in favour of secularity. Any constitution would
mean setting up some other law in opposition to the
Torah, ending the privileges enjoyed by the clerics,
notably by challenging the unconstitutional basis of
religious laws. Faced with the religious parties' intransigence, the other parties gave in, taking their lead from
the socialists.

The famous 'Law of Return' passed in 1950 gave
citizenship rights to any Jews who wished to make their
home in Israel. Along with this went the semi-automatic
granting of Israeli citizenship by virtue of the 1952
Nationality Act. But who is Jewish? The Israeli population
register lists three elements: religion, ethnic origins and
nationality. How can these categories be applied to Jews?
The Rufeisen and Chalitt affairs underlined the problem.
In the first case the Israeli Supreme Court refused to
acknowledge the ethnicity and to grant Israeli nationality
to a Jewish convert to catholicism. In the second case the
court decided to take Jewish ethnicity away from the
children of a Jewish father married to a non-Jew. But
according to Talmudic Law 'A Jew is someone who has a

Jewish mother or is a convert'. After long argument the Knesset accepted this when it ratified Article 42 of the Law of Return, which states that a Jew is someone who has a Jewish mother or is a convert and does not belong to any other faith. The Israeli Rabbinate go further: they do not accept conversions carried out by conservative or reformed Rabbis, which means that, in the final analysis, the sole arbiters of who is a Jew and therefore who has Israeli nationality are, *de facto*, the Rabbinic Courts.

The same thing is true of marriage. Israeli law follows the Ottoman and mandate examples in making the legal position in marriage and divorce dependent on the religion of the people concerned. 1953 legislation stated that 'the law applicable to marriage and divorce in Israel is the law of the Torah'. Since marriage between Jew and non-Jew is forbidden by divine law, then according to the lawyer Claude Klein 'It is impossible to contract a marriage between a Jew and a non-Jew in Israel'. There is no civil marriage in Israel so couples who have enough money go abroad to marry and on their return have their marriage registered 'automatically'.

Similarly, the main rules of religious observance are obligatory for everyone including atheists. Respect of the weekly Sabbath is ensured by a whole range of laws which prohibit all forms of public activity. Businesses, offices, shops, cafes, places of entertainment, restaurants, public transport, all close down. Even television is off the air. More recently rows have broken out over Saturday flights by El Al, the state airline. The highly complex regulations regarding kosher food, mainly to do with the absolute separation of meat and dairy produce, are respected throughout the economy, and cover the military as well as the civilian sectors. Very few restaurants ignore them for fear of being boycotted. Religious influence is so great that both the production and importation of pork are illegal.

The 1953 legislation also placed education within the sphere of religious influence. A law passed in 1959 included a guarantee to provide religious education for all children whose parents requested it. As a result two networks of schools exist side-by-side. Two thirds of pupils attend secular schools, but Bible and Talmud teaching still

figure prominently in the curriculum. The other third go
to religious schools. Over and above this there are the
yeshivah – the Agudat Orthodox Jews' schools. There are
between 350 and 400 of them, with between 22,000 and
25,000 pupils. State subsidies run into hundreds of dollars
per pupil per year.

This gives some idea of the extent of the Grand
Rabbinate's prerogatives, formalised by legislation in 1953
and again in 1980. It is a state body, financed by the state
and composed of one Ashkenazi Grand Rabbi and one
Sephardi Grand Rabbi. In addition to its purely religious
duties, the Rabbinical Council administers the Holy
Places, helps to monitor religious and secular education,
and keeps an eye on local Rabbinical courts, whose judges,
like those in other courts, are appointed by the state
president.

The excessive weight given to the power of religion was
enshrined in legislation in 1948 and reaffirmed in 1959.
The state was obliged to maintain the religious status quo.
This status quo was shattered by the 1977 coalition
break-up and realignment, which benefitted the Likud
and brought about the victory of Menachem Begin. The
demands made by the National Religious Party and
Agudat Israel in liaison with increasingly influential
religious and extremist nationalist groups like the Gush
Emunim were greater than ever before: more controls
over abortion, stricter observance of the Sabbath, a ban on
autopsies, the prohibition of archaeological digs in the
Holy Places, increased subsidies for the *yeshivah* colleges,
the introduction of religious law into Israeli legislation,
and so on. The Likud government reacted by agreeing to
everything, so long as public opinion went along with it.
No fewer than 70 of the 82 points in the 1981 coalition
agreement dealt with religious problems.

And yet, despite all this, the religious parties, who often
seem to be on a par with the much maligned ayatollahs,
could only manage 11.8% of the votes in the 1981 election.
And the all-powerful Rabbis' claims to represent all Israeli
Jews are seen to have little justification by opinion polls
which most recently showed that only 30% of the
population consider themselves religious or very religious,

45% consider themselves secular whilst respecting a few traditions and 25% say they are not religious in any way at all.

'The Black Problem'

The Declaration of Independence says that 'the State of Israel ... will maintain complete equality of social and political rights for all its citizens, without distinction of creed, race or sex'. As far as the Arabs are concerned this has been an empty promise, as we have already noted, and shall see again in chapter three. But they are not the only people who are still waiting for this undertaking to be fulfilled: so are the Afro-Asian Jews.

They are normally called Sephardim, but this is a mistake. In Hebrew Spharad means Spanish. Originally the Sephardim were Jews expelled from Spain and Portugal in 1492 and 1496 who went to live in exile all over the Mediterranean, in Italy, Greece, the Ottoman Empire and North Africa. Others went northwards to France, the Netherlands and Germany, some even crossed the Atlantic to the New World. The overwhelming majority of Oriental Jews in Israel have come from Arab countries and very few have Sephardim forebears. It is not just an unfortunate mix-up from a scientific viewpoint. It results in political errors: the traditions, culture and customs of the 'real' Sephardim are in fact much closer to Western than to Oriental Jews. Oriental Jews have almost nothing in common with those from the West. They come from underdeveloped, semi-feudal countries where for the most part they were involved in craft and commerce. Their standard of education is very low. They are often tied up with their religious traditions and have very limited political awareness. This can be explained by the weakness of the democratic movements in their old countries, and of course they have no revolutionary background. All of these elements explain their reasons for migrating to 'The Holy Land'.

For their benefit Zionists depicted the creation of the state of Israel as the realisation of a biblical promise. The anti-Jewish riots which took place in Arab countries after

Population of Israel (1981)

TOTAL	: 3,977,900
of which Jews	: 83.5%
non-Jews	: 16.5%

TOTAL JEWISH POPULATION	: 3,320,350
Born in Israel	: 57%
of whom parents born in Israel	: 14.9%
Asia	: 13.3%
Africa	: 12.4%
America	: 16.5%
Born in Africa or Asia	: 19.1%
Born in Europe or America	: 23.9%

TOTAL NON-JEWISH POPULATION	: 675,550
of which Muslims	: 78.1%
Christians	: 13.9%
Druze and others	: 8%

TOTAL ACTIVE CIVILIAN POPULATION	: 1,348,500 (i.e. 49.8% of those over 14 years old)	
TOTAL UNEMPLOYED	: 68,400 (i.e. 5.1%)	
WORKING POPULATION	: 1,128,100	
of which agricultural workers	: 6.1%	
industrial	: 23.4%	
water/electricity	: 1.1%	30.7%
construction	: 6.2%	
transport	: 6.7%	
commerce	: 12.0%	
financial	: 8.8%	63.2%
public services	: 30%	
private services	: 5.7%	
of which salaried workers	: 78.1%	
women	: 36.3%	
non-Jews	: 10.4%	

Source: Statistical Abstract of Israel 1982.

the partition of Palestine and which worsened during the 1948-49 fighting undermined the relative security they had enjoyed there for centuries. Although the *Dhimmi* (living under Islam) may have been humiliating for Jews, there was never any Arab equivalent of Auschwitz, Buchenwald and Dachau, a fact which some people readily overlook. And what the announcement of the Messiah's reign, and the fear of violence, could not do, the Israeli

Secret Service could: they hatched murderous plots. Massive Jewish emigration – the 'Ali Baba Operation' – followed the 1950 attack on the Shem Tov synagogue in Baghdad. Before that the 'Flying Carpet Operation' had 'lifted' most Jews out of Yemen.

For Oriental Jews the nation they found in Israel was very strange. They had nothing in common with either the Western, or Ashkenazi, Jews who had the top jobs in all sectors of the economy or with Zionist ideology, and even less with the 'socialist' form of Zionism. Little by little their numbers grew, from 25% of the Jewish population in 1948 to 50% in the 1960s, by which time the burden of discrimination they had endured during the *Yishuv* period, and at the beginning of the new state, had become intolerable. The second and third generations reacted against what their parents had passively accepted. The long established wall of silence surrounding them came crashing down in the clashes which took place in the Wadi Salib area of Haifa in 1959. In the 1960s there was a series of wildcat strikes. The 1970s gave rise to the Black Panther Movement. There was so much concern about this 'Second Israel' that the government appointed a commission of enquiry in 1974. The horrifying situation revealed in the Katz Report remains by and large the same in Israel today.

Segregation exists in all fields. Firstly in the sphere of work: among European and American born Jews 39% are craft or manual workers, and 14% occupy managerial or professional positions. The figures for Jews born in Africa and Asia are significantly different: 62% and 5% respectively. For the second generation the gap is wider: the figures for the sons of Western Jews are 24% and 17% in each category, while for the sons of Oriental Jews they come to 55% and 2%. Salary differences, together with the substantially higher number of children in Oriental families, reduce the Oriental *per capita* income to about half that of the Ashkenazim. There is also segregation in housing. On leaving the 'transit camps' the Oriental Jews were bundled into shanty towns. Average numbers of people per housing unit are: Ashkenazim 2.95, Sephardim 3.56, Arab 6.42. One of the many consequences of this is that the bulk of delinquents are Sephardim: 90% of common law prisoners and people with criminal records come from their community.

The continued existence of this gulf is certainly the most serious aspect of what the Ashkenazim call the 'black problem', which in itself is not entirely devoid of racist overtones. Education has something to do with it: 'We have succeeded in perpetuating the educational gulf from one generation to another', according to Arieh Eliav in a special issue of *Temps Modernes* dealing with the Second Israel. He goes on to argue that 'this failure effects the whole Zionist undertaking'. A few figures illustrate what he means: 41% of Ashkenazim go on to secondary education, whereas the Oriental figure is 16.8%, of whom 30.8% undertake vocational training, as against 23.2% of Ashkenazim. The proportions going on to study at university are worse: 13.8% of Ashkenazim and 2.8% of Orientals. The very low number of mixed marriages, only 17%, also contributes to the perpetuation of differences. The notion of 'acculturisation' has also played a role in excluding Oriental Jews from an Ashkenazi-dominated society. The arrogant demand made by Abba Eban, that Oriental Jews 'be taught Western values rather than be allowed to spread their unnatural habits', reflects this.

In the political sphere Ashkenazi hegemony is rock-solid: in 1981 they had 85% of ministers, 75% of the seats in the Knesset, nearly 90% of the members of the executive committees of both the Labour and Herut Parties and 75% of the executive of the Histadrut.

In his book *In the Land of Israel* the writer Amos Oz reported this comment made to him by an Oriental Jew.

'Think about this. When I was a little kid my kindergarten teacher was white and her assistant was black. In training. In school my teacher was Iraqi and the principal was Polish. On the construction site where I worked, my supervisor was some redhead from Soleh Boneh. At the clinic the nurse is Egyptian and the doctor Ashkenazi. In the army we Moroccans are the corporals and the officers are from the kibbutz. All my life I've been on the bottom and you've been on the top ... You brought our parents here to be your Arabs.'

The political aspects of the Oriental Jewish question

were underestimated and even ignored for a long time, but they came to the fore in 1977. In their eyes who was responsible for their position? Who could they react against? Who suppressed their demonstrations? Answer? The people who had been in power since 1948, and right back to 1935. The Socialist Zionists. Over the years the Labour Party had come to represent Ashkenazi oppression. That was enough to induce them to vote in large numbers for Menachem Begin, ignoring the fact the Likud was just as Ashkenazi-dominated as the Labour Party. In so doing they propelled the Israeli Right to electoral victory.

Socialism or Capitalism

Another Jewish joke – but then humour is a long-established feature of Jewishness, going back to the self-derision typical of the Yiddish ghettos: so, two Parisian Jews, Moshe and Isaac, bump into each other. They haven't seen each other for a long time. 'And your eldest boy? What's he doing now?' asks Moshe. 'He's in the Soviet Union' Isaac replies. 'And what's he doing there?' 'Building socialism.' 'And your other boy?' 'He's in Bulgaria.' 'Oh yes?' 'Building socialism.' And so on for all Isaac's children, they are all building socialism somewhere or other. Suddenly Moshe remembers the youngest one, David. 'And what about David? Where's he?' 'In Israel.' 'Building socialism in Israel?' Isaac bursts out laughing: 'Socialism? In our country? You must be joking!' The Isaac character in this famous joke would have a good laugh looking at the countless writings which set out to prove that Israel has its own brand of socialism. Some of them even put it forward as a model for others. There seems to be some sort of sleight-of-hand involved in all this. Let's try to see what it is, and unravel the mystery.

In many ways Israeli society does not fit into the classical framework of capitalism. First of all there is the anomaly of land ownership: according to property law, land, houses, apartment blocks, and any permanently fixed building, belongs to the state property service. It owns the freehold of 90% of the land in the country and leases part of it to farmers and local authorities. The only exceptions

are the Holy Places, some land bought before independence and the rare Arab dunams which have avoided
being bought out. Make of it what you will: as far as land
and building speculation are concerned Israel has nothing
to learn from the capitalist countries.

The second anomaly is collectivised farming. There are
235 kibbutzim, with 113,700 members who make up 30%
of the rural Jewish population and 3.4% of the national
total. There is plenty of literature available singing the
praises of their work and 'communist' lifestyle so we will
not spend a lot of time on it here. Seen from the inside the
kibbutzim certainly appear to bear out the maxim 'from
each according to his ability, to each according to his
needs'. Apart from personal effects, everything is
theoretically placed in common ownership under collective administration, including, as is well known, the
education of children. What those who extol the virtues of
these 'bastions of communism' leave out is the fact that the
kibbutzim are dependent on the banks, as well as their
other relations with the world outside. In addition to their
agricultural activity, most kibbutzim run small industrial
or semi-industrial businesses in which workers are
exploited – and in general it is Arabs that are being
exploited by Jews. Alongside the kibbutzim there are also
the *moshavim* which have 153,000 members representing
40% of rural Jews. These are very similar to cooperatives:
each family has its own house and is allocated a piece of
land. Earnings are linked to output. Like the kibbutzim,
the *moshavim* are affiliated together through various
national federations which are often linked to political
parties. Overall planning and co-ordination is carried out
by a central federation. The kibbutz, once at the very heart
of the reality and mythology of Israel, the breeding
ground of the country's socialist leaders – an institution
that it was virtually impossible to attack – now has to bear
the full force of a crisis that is more than just economic and
political: the very ideals of Zionism are in crisis.

The third anomaly is the Histadrut. The uniqueness of
the Histadrut, which we have already noted in the early
history of the *Yishuv*, has continued up to the present day.
Through the kibbutzim and moshavim which are linked to

it, the trade union confederation produces 70% of Israel's total agricultural output. This is distributed through its sales co-operative, the Tnuva. Its marketing organisation, the Hamashbir Hamerkazi, caters for the needs of a third of the population in its branches and supermarkets. 16% of national industrial output is achieved by the Histadrut's industrial sector, the Hevrat Ovdim (Society of Workers). The Koor is prominent in heavy industry; its 220 production and service cooperatives are involved in fields such as light metallurgical industry, wood and printing. The Solel Boneh, which belongs to it, accounts for 30% of construction companies (with a few smaller companies). Nearly 400.000 Israelis live in Histadrut-built homes. It also owns the second largest bank in the country, the Ha-Poalim, and the largest insurance company, the Hassneh, and partly controls the two most important transport businesses, the Egged and Dan cooperatives. As well as being the largest employer in the country the Histadrut is also the greatest provider of health care: 75% of the population are covered by its health insurance company, the Kupat Holim, which runs a network of hospitals, clinics, dispensaries, rest homes and so on.

Putting it all together, the agricultural, industrial, commercial and service companies linked to the Histadrut are responsible for nearly 30% of Israel's economic activity and approximately 28% of G.N.P. More than two thirds of farmworkers, and nearly a quarter of all wage earners, are employed through the union, according to the 1977 figures which the Histadrut leadership have not been reluctant to make available.

These then are the component parts of 'Israeli Socialism', according to its apologists. But this rather overstates the case. The statistics themselves raise a number of questions. (Incidentally, they are carefully tucked away, right at the end of a table in the Statistical Abstract of Israel). Although the balance between collective and private enterprise in agriculture is 70% versus 30% it is the other way round in the industrial sector. Private companies employ 71.5% of industrial wage earners, as against the Histadrut's 11.6% and the public sector's 16.9%. Indeed the very idea of the existence of a public sector is questionable: apart from a few exceptions such as armaments, aerospace and electricity, the state shares ownership of its industries with the Hevrat Ovdim, and to an even greater extent with private capital. Experience has shown who does best out of this type of mixed ownership. The private sector is even more firmly in control of services, shops and, of course, of finance.

But this is not just an argument about figures, or about who owns what. The point is this: who runs the state, and who for? Linked to this is another question which is just as significant: where does the Histadrut's activity fit in?

Put plainly, Israel's economic structure has been turned upside down by the same process of concentration of finance and industrial capital that has gone on in all the other capitalist countries. If Israel is atypical it is so only because of the effects of war and, since 1967, occupation, which have both accentuated and speeded up the process. In Israel today it is not just jargon to say that a handful of people run three quarters or even four fifths of the economy. They are so closely involved with the state apparatus and are in such a hegemonic position in industry that the directors of these monopolies are able to do whatever they want. Their way of thinking, geared to instant profit, predominates in the public and private sectors, and even in the Histadrut to some extent. The leaders of the Trade Union Confederation had no hesitation in calling on their members to collaborate with the capitalists in the name of 'class harmony', 'economic responsibility', and 'national unity' in face of the enemy. In so doing they have been caught up in a web of support for militarism and colonialism, and their authority has been compromised. The 1977 Likud victory completed the establishment of state monopoly capitalism in Israel and precipitated its crisis.

United Against the Enemy

Herzl's aim was to keep soldiers out of the affairs of state. This goes to show that no-one is a prophet in their own country. The parts played by Dayan, Weizman and Sharon on the Right, and by Rabin and Bar Lev on the Left, and even by the pacifist Peled, indicate just how clearly the generals have encroached upon the political domain and the state apparatus in Israel. Five wars and five victories has proved to be an irresistible argument.

The omnipresent influence of the army in Israeli society can not just be measured by the number of high-ranking officers who are made ministers or are appointed to leadership positions in the parties. The effects of the state of war between Israel and her neighbours on the country's economy, its democracy and its ideology have already been examined several times. At this point the influence of the armed forces on all aspects of Israeli life must be assessed.

'Every Israeli citizen is a soldier on leave.' Such was the claim made by the Chief of Staff of the Israeli Defence Force. It was by now means an exaggeration. Military service lasts three years for men and two years for unmarried women. In addition men up to the age of 55 and women up to 34 are called up as 'reservists' every year, for a minimum of 30 days, which can often be extended to 60, 90 or even 120 days at tense moments. In other words the average 56-year-old Israeli has spent between seven and eight years of his life in the army over and above any wartime service. The only people who are exempted are the Arabs, except the Druze, students at the *Yeshivahs* (religious colleges), and young women who take an oath of orthodoxy. This continuing involvement with the military is not without repercussions – delayed higher education and late entry onto the job market for example – but the ideological consequences are greater still. Many armies elsewhere in the world look longingly at the length of time available for the Israeli Defence Forces to 'mould' the young, both in the barracks and through its education network, which is the largest in the country and of course reflects army values. The Defence Force consumes 35% of G.N.P., over 50% of the budget; it accounts for half of all research and development spending. Other indices pointing to the economic weight of the Defence forces should be added to the above figures. It accounts for half of all Israeli imports – and it should be borne in mind that Israel is the world's number one importer. Bitter experience has taught the Arab peoples to recognise

Skyhawk and Phantom jets, Hawk missiles and Patton tanks, not to mention highly sophisticated bombs, all of which come from the United States. General de Gaulle's 1967 arms embargo spurred Israel on to build up its own, autonomous armaments industry producing such successes as the Kfir jet fighter, the Merkeva tank and high speed armed patrol boats. There is a long list of companies which supply the military with uniforms, electronic machinery, optics and so on. Overall there are tens of thousands of workers whose livelihood depends on orders from the military in this way. Strangely enough, Israel the arms importer has also become Israel the arms exporter; and high on the list of good customers come South Africa and almost all the Latin-American dictatorships.

For Israel the Defence Force represents power, honour, virtue and pride; every citizen is immersed in it from a very early age. Not doing military service is shameful and makes you a pariah. 'Profile 21' people, who are so called because of the law which applies to them, have difficulty in taking a driving test or obtaining work as civil servants or even getting a job at all. War and preparing for war occupy a central position in Israeli political and social culture.

For a long time the threat of destruction has acted to bring people together in defence of their country. It's almost as if the existence of a state of conflict is necessary for national unity. But this is a very dangerous state of affairs. The threat to Israel was imaginary – not because of the real or supposed intentions of Israel's enemies, but because of the balance of power. However, thanks to their leaders' propaganda, the Israelis felt that they were in danger in 1956 and in 1967, when in fact it was the Israeli army which was the aggressor. In their eyes the only guarantee of peace was the power of the Defence Forces.

But people started to see things more clearly after the Yom Kippur war. 'One fine day Superman woke up to discover that he was just like everyone else', according to Amnon Kapeliouk in *Israel: The End of the Myths*. This book analyses the post 1973 disillusionment with considerable finesse. Basically, says Kapeliouk, it was at this time that people stopped believing in the old myths of the supposedly eternal *status quo*, Israel's secure borders, the unchallenged invincibility of the Defence Forces and the proverbial infallibility of the secret services (Shin Bet, Aman and Mossad). They stopped believing that the Arabs did not have it in them to fight a war, that the Palestinians in the Gaza Strip and West Bank were 'resigned' to their lot, and that time was on Israel's side.

Nobody laughs any more at this anecdote which was very popular after the Six Day War: A government meeting is taking place. They are discussing how to get out of their awful economic difficulties. Declare war on the United States, suggests one minister. Everyone is surprised. But, he explains, look at Germany: they were at war with the Americans, they lost, and Washington gave them thousands of millions of dollars in order to rebuild. Moshe Dayan then says, 'But what if we win?' After the hammering the Israeli military took in the first few days of the Yom Kippur war the story now seems like a sick joke.

This process has been accentuated by the colonisation of the West Bank and still more so by the invasion of Lebanon. Many consciences, or at least many of the more enlightened consciences, have been troubled by what has happened, and doubts have arisen, even about the very legitimacy of what is going on. Proof of this can be seen in the split that has grown between the Jews in Israel and those in the diaspora. We shall return to this, but we can note here and now that Arieh Eliav's fears were justified: war, while still a unifying factor for many, is at the same time also having a contradictory effect: it is tending towards the destruction of Israel. Only time will tell how seriously, but Zionism has certainly been damaged.

The 'Left'

As we have seen Israeli society is riddled with a large number of highly dangerous contradictions. The class conflicts which are found in all capitalist societies are accompanied by other tensions which war and occupation have exacerbated: the conflicts between religious and lay interests, between Oriental and Western Jews and between authoritarianism and democracy. The economy is bankrupt and only survives thanks to transfusions of American

capital. The confidence of the past has given way to
uncertainty and insecurity. An ever-increasing surge of
complaint has swept the country.

Who is responsible? The Israeli voters were quite clear
on this question: the Labour Party has paid an increasingly
high price for past failures. The figures below show the
aggregate percentage of the vote achieved in Knesset
elections by the Mapai and the Mapam, the Rafi splinter
group of 1965, the Ahdut Ha-Avodah and the affiliated
Arab lists. They show the extent of the decline in support
for the Labour Alignment from 1965 onwards:

1949	1951	1955	1959	1961	1965	1969	1973	1977
53.4%	50.9%	51%	55.3%	52.3%	54.5%	49.7%	42.1%	26%

This decline in support is no less striking in the
percentage achieved in the preparatory consultations for
Histadrut Congresses in the same period, even though the
Histadrut is supposed to be a bastion of socialism:

1949	1955	1959	1965	1969	1973	1977
93.61%	86.95%	87.95%	77.51%	65.17%	62.56%	58.01%

It is true that the exercise of power can be wearing. But
the socialists were in charge of the *Yishuv* from the 1930s
onwards, and in government from the birth of the state of
Israel. The events which occurred were not a result of
things simply taking their course without the intervention
of the government: what happened was largely their
responsibility. What the electorate rejected, then, was the
Labour Alignment's political strategy.

The Six Day war, and to a much greater extent the Yom
Kippur war hastened the process of political disillusionment. The leaders of the Labour Party seemed to be
such war-mongers that their voters deserted them: the
most chauvinist elements, who had been worried by the
1973 'Arab break-through', moved to the right; while the
pacifist wing was demobilised. Meanwhile those on the
lowest rungs of the social ladder, largely Oriental Jews,
blamed Labour for their poverty and, driven on by their
despair, fell into the arms of the Likud.

Matters were made worse by a crisis within the socialist movement itself. Decades of power had turned the Labour Party into a party of the well-off: its support, which in the past had come from the working class, was now made up of civil servants and the middle class. Party organisation was stifled by bureaucratic inertia and mounting tensions. After Golda Meir's retirement there was no recognised leader and the subsequent battles for succession did little for the reputation of either the party or the contestants themselves. Clashes between hawks and doves were forced out of the limelight just before the 1977 elections by the public's passionate interest in the details of financial scandals involving ministers and Labour leaders. Itzhak Rabin himself was charged with the illegal export of currency.

The killer blow for the Labour Party was when an insignificant third force, the D.A.S.H. (Democratic Movement for Change) exploded on the political scene. In 1977 it obtained 11.6% of the votes, taking most of them from the Left. Before it ceased to exist the D.A.S.H. came to terms with the Likud and joined the government coalition.

Popular desire for change took the form of a move to the right, but in part that was because there was no credible alternative to the Labour Party. The Left within the Labour Party itself was trapped by the heavy hand of the party bureaucracy. And there were problems in the smaller left parties. The Mapam had inherited an interesting position from its predecessors: support for a bi-national state and friendship with the Soviet Union, coupled with strong roots in the kibbutzim. But its entry into government in 1967 and its incorporation into the Labour Party-controlled Maarakh Front considerably reduced its field of manoeuvre. Until 1981 its position was the same as the Labour Party's. As far as the non-Labour, non-Communist Left is concerned it was made up of many, many tiny groups continually splintering and merging and had no effective impact at all until the emergence of the pacifist movement which we shall look at later on. At its peak in 1973 this section of the left had no more than four members of the Knesset: between them,

the Moked, Uri Avneri's Ha-Olam Ha-Zeh and Shulamith
Aloni's Civil Rights Movement only accounted for 4.3% of
the votes cast.

The courage – often physical – commitment and interna-
tionalism shown by communist activists have not been
enough to break down the barriers of ostracism which
surround their party. Anti-zionists in a Zionist state, supporters of a Palestinian state – unthinkable to the majority
of Israelis – as well as of the Soviet Union, which was
thought of as an 'Evil Empire' in Israel long before President Reagan used the term, the Communist Party of Israel
is of course portrayed as a 'foreign body'. The consequences of the 1965 split which created two parties were
grave: the Maki, which was less anti-zionist, went into
decline, while the Rakah remained as the Israeli representative in the communist movement. However the electoral
and organisational bi-nationalism of the Rakah was seriously undermined by the split, and most of its activists and
its electoral support now come from the Israeli Arab community. Support hovered around 4% until the split when it
fell to between 2% and 3%, but rose again to between 3%
and 4% when the Rakah joined other groups, and notably a
group of 'Black Panthers' in forming the Haddash (Democratic Front for Peace and Equality). The long, painstaking
work of the party can be seen as one of the elements that
sparked off the pacifist explosion in 1982.

It can be said, then, that the Likud owes its rise to power
just as much to the lack of any left-wing alternative as to the
electorate's rejection of the Labour Party. As the graph
shows, the rise of the Right is just as steady as the demise of
the Left. The following statistics show the combined votes
polled for the Herut and the Liberal Party (but not the
independent liberals), and then the Gahal Coalition in 1965
and 1969, and the Likud in 1977. General Sharon's small
group Schlomzion (Peace of Zion) is included in 1977.

1949	1951	1955	1959	1961	1965	1969	1973	1977
16.7%	22.8%	22.8%	19.7%	27.4%	21.3%	21.7%	30.2%	35.3%

Likud support in the Histadrut grew likewise: from
11.85% in 1969, it rose to 22.74% in 1973 and to 28.60% in
1977.

Voting Patterns 1949-81

Number of seats
in Parliament

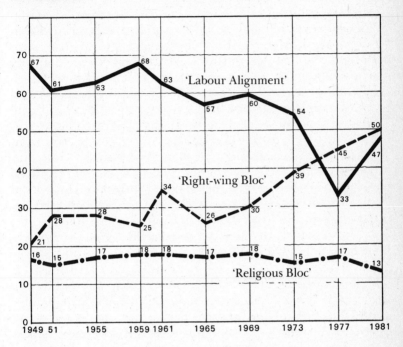

The figures indicate the total number of seats obtained by each of the three main political alignments in the ten Knesset elections:

Labour Alignment: Mapai, Ahdut Ha-Avodah, and Mapam, which subsequently combined to become the Maarakh Front, plus the Arab lists allied to the Labour Party. (Votes received by Labour dissidents, the extreme left and Communists are not included).

Right Wing Bloc: initially the Herut and the Liberal Party – but not the independent Liberals. These subsequently combined to form the Gahal, which then became the Likud. This figure also includes votes for extreme right groups such as Schlomzion and the Tehial.

Religious Bloc: Mafdal (National Religious Party), Agudat Israel and Poale Agudat Israel.

There was nothing sudden about the 'historic turn-ing point' of 1977. The Right did not just try to win over the voters who felt let down by Israeli socialism. It cast its nets in all directions hoping to catch anybody and everybody, with the bait adjusted accordingly. Begin offered a 'strong-arm' hard-line colonising and annexa-tionist policy to those whose nationalist feelings had been aroused by the Yom Kippur war. To the Oriental or Sephardim Jews he promised equality tomorrow in terms that were anti-Ashkenazi and had racist overtones. He bought the support of the religious parties by dangling the idea of a theocracy in front of them. He offered 'miracle' answers to the problems faced by all the victims of the economic crisis. Ronald Reagan and Margaret Thatcher were later to have great success with a similar strategy. Finally the former terrorist used – and abused – his charisma: he was the last surviving leader of 'The Jewish People'.

The Begin Era

The coming to power of Begin represents a break in the political history of the state of Israel. It marked the end of decades of Labour hegemony and conferred legitimacy on a party, a tendency, of people who had long been called 'fascists' by their opponents. From the morning of 18 May 1977 when the country woke up to find it had a right-wing government a new joke went the rounds:

Question: What's the difference between Israel and a lunatic asylum?

Answer: In a lunatic asylum the administration is at least sane.

While not mad, the new masters in Tel Aviv personified Israel at its most retrograde, chauvinist and extremist. The facts speak for themselves. There is little room for a favourable interpretation of the Likud after the experi-ence of their years in government.

Menachem Begin's Israel began to flex its muscles. From the outset it rushed headlong into implementing its adventurist policies: dozens of new colonies and repress-ion in the Gaza Strip and on the West Bank, intervention in Southern Lebanon, raids on Iraq, the annexation of East Jerusalem and the Golan Heights. Finally, and above all, came the invasion of Lebanon and the occupation of the southern part of the country. What remained of the country's economic resources was used up in these adventures. The cost was astronomical: in 1984 the occupation of Lebanon gobbled up a million dollars a day, and the colonisation of Arab lands came to a billion dollars over the year.

To get the funds to pay for their foreign policy, the right-wing coalition imposed a 'free-market liberalism' on the country: subsidies and removal of financial controls for the big companies, wage freezes for the workers, cuts in welfare budgets and attempts at denationalisation. The figures make grim reading. The inflationary spiral from 1981 onwards speaks volumes: 132.9% in 1980, 101.9% in 1981, 131% in 1982, 190.7% in 1983, and so on. Unemployment, which had been low in the past, climbed to over 5% of the workforce in 1981. As has already been noted external debt smashed all records. The dollar, worth six Israel pounds in 1974, traded at 25 to the pound in 1979, 150 in 1981 and 1600 in April 1984. The purchasing power of wages and pensions collapsed. Some say that it fell by 40% in 1983. The social welfare budget was cut so drastically that it led to the government crisis of March 1984 which in turn led to early elections in July that year.

The most obvious symptom of the chaos caused by the economic stagnation is that, beginning in the second half of the 1970s, there has been a growing tide of people leaving Israel for good. Year in, year out, more people are emigrating than immigrating. An average of 15,000 people per year are going.

But Israel is not a country like other countries: a Jew who leaves is deserting 'The Promised Land', the state set up for those who 'escaped genocide', the Jewish refuge. Quite apart from the economic worries, the emigration figures reflect a crisis of identity which has shaken Zionism. Israel Harel, President of the Settlements Committee in 'Judea and Samaria' and Gaza, a Gush Emunim activist, put it quite cynically to Amos Oz: 'The main difference is between Jews and Israelis. The Jews are people who wish to live more or less according to the law of the Torah. The Israelis are happy to pay lip service to tradition but really want to become a new people in a Western satellite country ... their presence in this state is just a biographical accident, nothing more ... If a better alternative could be offered them the other side of the sea they would move'.

These remarks made by an extremist leader conceal the other politico-psychological factors which induce people to leave. Certainly no-one would doubt that material insecurity counts, but so also does fear of a never-ending conflict, with no idea of where it might lead. 'When they hear the word 'value' they get out their cheque books.' This quip from a character in Rachel Mizrahi's book *One dies, so does the other* points to another aspect of the problem: the erosion of the Zionist ideal. The haggling which has become a national pastime, the frenzied consumerism and contempt for manual labour, the fact that able minds are allowed to lie idle, together with the increasing prevalence of delinquency, all go to show just how badly Israel has 'blown it'. Neither the reality of Israel today, nor the country's role in Middle Eastern affairs, can honestly be equated, if not with Zionism, then with the hopes of the pioneers. This is without doubt a key factor in the concern about relations with Israel which came to the surface in 1982 throughout the diaspora. Jews abroad, like Jews in Tel Aviv, no longer hesitate about making their disagreement with Israeli policy public knowledge.

The last of the Likud's achievements was the unprecedented isolation of Israel within the world community. Diplomatic relations had been severed with the socialist countries except Rumania since 1967. The majority of African and Asian countries had long ago severed links with Tel Aviv. But most of all the Begin era saw Israel discredited in Latin America and in the eyes of Western public opinion. On occasion the Israeli representatives at the U.N. found themselves on their own with the U.S.A. against the rest of the world. As Israel became more isolated so Washington increased its support. Over a period of time reciprocal dependence has come to be the hallmark of Israeli-American relations. The two partners argue from time to time but neither of them would ever or could ever contemplate a break-up.

This awful record did not stop the Likud winning the 1981 elections which all the opinion polls said Labour would win with ease. A popular joke at the time says more than detailed analyses about this remarkable turn of events:

One day Abraham was in a state. He buttonholed Samuel at the corner of Dizengoff Avenue and poured out his heart: 'I'm off, I've had enough of this b ... country!'

'But why?' asked Samuel.

'Two reasons. One: that fascist Begin with his generals and his rabbis, I just can't put up with his awful policies any longer ... '

Samuel butts in: 'Well, hold on a bit: Shimon Peres and Co will be back in power soon.'

Abraham cuts him short: 'That's the second reason why I'm going.'

This joke captures in a nutshell the main reason why the Likud Coalition managed to cling onto power in 1981 despite its heavy liabilities: there was no left-wing alternative since the Labour Party had shown no sign of renewing either its programme or its organisation. In these circumstances it was easy for Menachem Begin and his people to make the most of their one big achievement: Camp David. It served a dual purpose for the Likud: when appealing to the nationalist voters they could put themselves forward as having forced the Arabs to negotiate and – what was more – on Israeli terms. To the moderates they had been the first to make some progress towards peace. With the addition of a few last minute vote-catching antics such as the bombing of Tamuz, a few eye-catching price cuts and massive imports of consumer goods the election was in the bag.

However this fragile victory was soon brought into question by the operation known as 'Peace in Galilee'. Did Ariel Sharon, who both devised and implemented the plan to invade Lebanon, *really* hope to manage in a short time both to be done with the P.L.O. once and for all, and to establish a Christian government in Beirut which would be

willing to sign a sort of Camp David II, for the north? In
any case, the fact of the matter is that he did not do so. The
P.L.O. managed to get out of Beirut and although
weakened by battle and by internal divisions continues to
play an important role in Middle Eastern affairs. The
dream of a Phalangist state negotiating with Tel Aviv
vanished in the Syrian-backed Lebanese armed forces'
uprising. So the aims of the invasion were not fulfilled and
the 'lightning attack' became an interminable conflict.

It did not take long for this to boomerang, with
consequences that the Likud sorcerer's apprentices had
certainly never thought of. The Israelis were used to wars
that were over in a few days. They now had to meet the
cost of an occupying army contending with active
resistance: billions of dollars and hundreds of deaths, not
to mention the universal condemnation of the massacres
in the Sabra and Shatila camps. The war accentuated the
country's social, political, moral and economic crisis to
such an extent that it reached previously unheard of
proportions. It led to two developments in Israel from
1982 onwards: a social movement which brought together
one after another all the liveliest forces in the country to
condemn the government's austerity programme, and a
pacifist movement which was powerful, heterogenous, and
deeply based in the grass roots. No one will ever forget the
400,000 strong demonstration against the massacres: it
was as though five million people had gathered in Paris to
show their feelings about one or other of the horrors
committed in Algeria. Nor will people forget the Yech
Gvul movement ('There is a limit') of soldiers refusing to
serve in Lebanon. The economy was bankrupt, the army
was bogged down in South Lebanon, Egypt had
abandoned the Camp David process, demonstrations had
been organised by workers and pacifists: it was all too
much for Menachem Begin's successor Itzhak Shamir,
whose administration suffered a vote of censure on 19
March 1984.

Were the 24 July elections decisive? They would have
been on one condition: that the Labour Party end the
underlying consensus that linked it to the Likud and
presented itself as offering a real alternative, in which the

social and peace movements could at last come together in common cause. It is not possible to separate crisis, war and occupation. The only solution to Israel's problems would involve withdrawal from Lebanon and the occupied territories. This would then allow a drastic reduction in the military expenditure budget, which is having a crushing effect on the economy. In fact they can only get by thanks to American aid and draconian austerity measures. But this is an analysis that Shimon Peres was not willing to put forward in the election campaign, the Labour Party preferring to fight on the Likud's terms and hoping to outdo them. Given this lack of perspective there was no channel for the political awareness that had arisen from the Lebanese war: the Likud and the Labour Alignment ended up on similiar ground, dependent on the religious parties, while a small proportion of the electorate became polarised, particularly on the far right where the symbolic electoral victory of Rabbi Kahane was a worrying development.

A government of national unity with alternative prime ministers was on the cards throughout the election campaign, and was the logical outcome when the results were known. In purely arithmetical terms neither party was able to form a coalition without being at the mercy of the religious parties, so it was only logical for them to join forces round the table. It was also politically logical: the Likud and the Labour Party basically agreed on domestic and foreign policy so they were able to govern together. Such were the origins of a hybrid form of government which has, until now, proved shock-resistant, although it is true that it has mostly been engaged in non-contentious issues such as withdrawing the armed forces from Lebanon and implementing increased austerity programmes.

Withdrawal from Lebanon has been made to synchro-nise with the deployment in the buffer zone of General Lahad's forces, which are Israeli-trained and equipped and have Israeli 'advisers'. The Amal militia meanwhile keep a tight hold on the south and on Beirut to ensure that any resurgence of Palestinian activity is nipped in the bud. Despite the extremely painful austerity measures there has not yet been any orchestrated opposition; doubtless people accept them because there does not seem to be any practical alternative. The prospect of negotiations with the Jordanians and Palestinians presents more of a problem. Although both coalition partners refuse to talk to the P.L.O. or to envisage the creation of a Palestinian state, they had different positions on what 'territorial concessions' they would be prepared to make: Shamir refuses to yield so much as an inch of the occupied territories while Peres says he is prepared to return 'some of it' – to Jordan.

Are the seeds of break-up of the national coalition to be found here? On this issue, as with anything else to do with future Israeli policy, it would be unwise to give too categorical an answer: basic decisions in Tel Aviv are subject to far too many interlinked influences and pressures for that. Pressure comes from the situation itself: the catastrophic crisis in Israeli society means that cosmetic measures are useless, and that in the long-run radical answers will be sought, which may either be negative – some form of fascism perhaps – or positive – some kind of peaceful compromise. Another pressure comes from the P.L.O. and the Arab states: although their divisions make life easier for Israel's leaders, the prospect of a Palestinian resistance coming together behind a realistic proposal supported by their 'brothers', who are today silent as one calamity follows another, must give the Israelis pause for thought. The Americans too exert pressure: Israel has become so dependent on the White House that any change in American strategy could not fail to be influential to some degree. Lastly there is pressure from within: a renewed upsurge in the social and pacifist movements, which could take the form of a political grouping on the left of the Labour Party, and, through dialogue with the Palestinians, could put everything back to square one.

In June 1967, when the communists were virtually alone in condemning Israeli aggression, Maxime Rodinson wrote a famous article in *Le Monde* in which he stated that 'If there is any tradition in Jewish history it is the tradition of collective suicide'. He went on to add 'Pure aesthetes can admire its cruel beauty if they so wish. Perhaps we can point out, as Jeremiah did to those whose policies led to he destruction of the first temple, or as Yohanan Ben Zakkai did to those who caused the ruination of the third temple, that there is another path, no matter how difficult past policies have made it for us to take. Can we hope that those people who claim to be above all else builders and sowers will choose this path, the path of life?'

Chapter 3

The Palestinians

Zionists used to dismiss Palestine, asserting that it was 'a land without a people'. The history of the last 70 years has continually refuted their assertion. The Palestinians *do* exist and the Middle East has been dominated by their ordeal ever since that fateful day in 1922 when the League of Nations handed Britain a mandate over Palestine. They have disappeared, reappeared, and undergone exodus and exile. To use Yasser Arafat's expression they are like the phoenix, reborn out of its ashes. The Middle East has been turned into a minefield by the stubbornness of those who would deny the Palestinians their rights; who can tell if one day one of the Middle Eastern mines might not spark off a much larger explosion?

Palestine Under the Mandate

The area under the jurisdiction of the mandate covered 27,000 square kilometres, smaller than Belgium and only 2,000 square kilometres larger than Sicily. In 1922 its population was made up of 600,000 Muslims, 72,000 Christians and 84,000 Jews. The vast majority of the Arabs were Sunni Muslims, though there was a small Druze minority. The Christian Arabs were divided into many different sects. The largest group were Greek Orthodox, the rest belonged to one or other of the Roman Catholic communities with the exception of a few thousand Protestants. The Arab population was largely rural. In 1922 Jerusalem was the only town with more than 50,000 inhabitants. Although less than a quarter of the Arab population were city dwellers, more than three quarters of the Christian community were. Despite a degree of urban development under the mandate the Arab population remained concentrated in the rural areas.

On the eve of the First World War Palestinian economic and social organisation was semi-feudal. It was to undergo a twofold shake-up: being put under the control of a metropolitan colonial power, and witnessing the parallel development of a more advanced and dynamic society, the *Yishuv*, In 1931 59% of the Arab workforce were involved in agriculture. By 1945 this had fallen to 51% for a number of reasons: land purchased by Jews leading to the expulsion of the Palestinian peasants; migration into the towns; and gradual reduction in cereal cultivation in favour of citrus fruit – Palestine was becoming a single-crop economy in the interests of metropolitan profit.

The social structure in the countryside at the time is characterised by a wide gulf in ownership: in 1930 30% of the peasant families owned no land. 0.03% of the landowners owned large estates amounting to 27.4% of the land. A further 8% owned 35.8% of the land. The remaining 37.1% of the land was shared by 91.8% of the landowners. The great landowning families, who were chiefly Muslim, wielded very considerable influence in the countryside, where patronage dominated relations. A small number of families also exerted authority in the towns, but here Christians also played a significant role. An urban middle class comprising teachers, civil servants and intellectuals, whose interests were tied up with the state apparatus and local government, began to emerge. Clearly the working class is very weak in this kind of traditional economy. Thus the Palestinian National Movement grew up in an agrarian society dominated by colonialism.

Early Resistance and Setbacks

Right from the beginning of the 20th century the Palestinian national movement formed an integral part of the growing Arab national movement in the Middle East, though it was to acquire its own special character in the struggle against Jewish immigration and Zionism. The desire for unity with the rest of the Arab world coloured everything else after Allenby's troops reached Jerusalem in December 1917. Feisal, the son of Sharif Hussein, had taken power in Damascus. The idea of setting up, under his leadership, a kingdom of Greater Syria, which would include the future Palestine, seemed to echo united Arab aspirations and was certainly the best way of opposing the Balfour declaration. The Palestinian leaders changed direction, however, as a result of the fall of Feisal in July 1920, when French troops entered Damascus. Henceforward their struggle concentrated on Palestine until 1936.

From as early as 1921 the movement demanded the annulment of the Balfour declaration, and an end to Jewish immigration and land purchases by Zionist organisations. But support for these demands only partially concealed the splits existing between the important families involved in the leadership of the Palestinian Congress, which claimed to express the will of the people. There was a bitter power struggle involving the Nashashibi and Husseini clans. The fact that the feudal overlords were prepared to come to terms with Britain further weakened an organisation in which Muslim-Christian relations were far from perfect, while the British were of course eager to stir matters up. The end result of these contradictions was the break-up of the united Palestinian organisations and the setting up of numerous factions and parties. It was not until 1928 that the Palestinians overcame the impotence caused by this fragmentation.

Despite these factors a slow maturing went on. The new urban classes who were less tied to the clans started to take action. In the countryside the largest group in the population, the peasants, were becoming more radical as a consequence of expropriation. So as not to lose their influence some of the traditional leaders began to adopt a harder line. Thus, for example, the Mufti of Jerusalem, Hajj Amin Al Husseini, president of the Muslim High Council did not shrink from criticism of the British or from anti-Jewish propaganda. The August 1929 riots, which began in Jerusalem over control of the Jewish and Muslim Holy Places, but spread throughout Palestine, were an expression of different facets of the Palestinian movement. There were anti-Jewish pogroms, peasant uprisings and the first attacks on the mandatory authorities.

This process began to accelerate at the beginning of the 1930s, as Jewish immigration rose to new proportions. It culminated in the 1936-39 revolt. The spiritual father of the revolt was Izzeddin Qassem, the son of a peasant and a devout Muslim. He began to spread the word in Haifa and the surrounding area, forming clandestine cells for armed struggle (although he condemned the mindless violence of 1929). He was critical of the inertia of the official Palestinian organisations, and argued that Great Britain was the root of all their troubles. His appeal was to the common people and especially to the fellahs who were resisting Zionist expropriation and standing up to the big Arab landowners. He was killed in November 1935 after taking to the hills and calling for an insurrection; his funeral was the scene of a major demonstration. This was the nationalist and anti-imperialist atmosphere in the Middle East which served as a backcloth to the events of 1936.

British rejection of Palestinian demands led to a strike which spread throughout the country in April 1936. The traditional leaders added their support: an Arab Higher Committee, chaired by Amin Al Husseini, brought the different political forces together. The strike lasted for 170 days, to the accompaniment of a wave of civil disobedience, guerilla activity and peasant uprisings. Eventually, however, the High Committee issued a joint appeal from Saudi Arabia, Iraq and Transjordan calling for the suspension of the strike and for 'trust in the good intentions of our British friends'. Following this, the first instance of Arab involvement in Palestinian affairs, the revolt came to a provisional end. A British Royal Commission was set up to enquire into possible solutions. The report was published on 7 July 1937: it proposed to divide Palestine into two states.

The failure of negotiations with Britain acted as a spur

to the movement, which henceforward became popular, insurrectionist, anti-British and anti-feudal in character. The repression with which it was received was made worse by the direct involvement of Zionist groups and some of the great Palestinian families, notably the Nashashibis. Thousands of people died and hundreds were deported: the active elements of the Palestinian resistance were crushed. Its role was greatly reduced for the next 20 years – the time it took to recover from this blow. Amin Al Husseini maintained his anti-British stance, but discredited his people by seeking refuge in Nazi Germany. The suppression of the revolt gave birth to splits, animosity and hatred which were to last a long time. The gulf between the Jewish and Arab communities grew wider. The Communist Party of Palestine's attempt at united Arab-Jewish action against the policies of London had only very limited impact.

The crushed and disorganised Palestinian resistance came to rely increasingly on the Arab governments to put its case. The British government white paper of 1939 limiting Jewish immigration and land purchase as well as looking forward to the setting up of an independent Palestinian state was seen as a 'success' which was due to pressure from 'brother' countries. But the Arab monarchs in Egypt, Iraq and Transjordan were all heavily dependent on London. As far as Palestine was concerned each had their own ambitions as well as Britain's to further. After the Second World War, when Britain was forced to put the 'Palestinian Question' to the U.N., it manipulated the Arab states to ensure the failure of the 1947 partition plan. As we have seen Britain even incited them to go to war against the new Jewish state.

The Palestinian movement was dragged along in the wake of these policies, and later paid the price. Zionist terrorism and the defeat of the Arab armies precipitated the Palestinian population into flight. After the 1949 armistice, more than half the Arabs in Palestine sought refuge either in Gaza or Jordan or on the east bank of the River Jordan, in Lebanon or in Syria. Not only did the Arab state planned by the U.N. never see the light of day but the Palestinian people had to witness the carve-up of the parts of their lands which were under Arab control. In mid-December 1948 the King of Transjordan proclaimed himself King of Palestine and went on to annex the West Bank. The remnants of the Arab Higher Committee, still chaired by Amin Al Husseini, set themselves up in Gaza and formed a government which was recognised by the Arab League. It represented no one but itself, was under Arab protection, and was to disappear, to everyone's indifference. For the Palestinians the situation was catastrophic: their land had been 'annexed' on the West Bank, in Lebanon they were muzzled, Gaza was like a high security prison, and there was a military government in Israel. Their society was falling apart. Herded together under canvas in conditions of appalling deprivation they endeavoured to survive. The most politicised elements, convinced they had been betrayed by the Arabs, for the most part became involved in the battles which over the next ten years changed the face of the Middle East: the fall of King Farouk of Egypt in 1952, the failure of the Anglo-French-Israeli Suez expedition in 1956, the fall of the Iraqi monarchy in 1958 and so on. But the Palestinian question as such was ignored. It only came up in passing, in inflammatory speeches by Arab leaders. For a while it even seemed to have gone away for good ... as though it were that easy to just wipe a people off the map.

The P.L.O.

It is May 1964 in Jerusalem. In a few hours the Palestinian National Congress is going to start: it will bring the Palestine Liberation Organisation into being. Its future president, Ahmed Shukeiri begs King Hussein to attend the opening session. The Hashemite king finally agrees but on two conditions: that the future P.L.O. should undertake not to organise or arm the Palestinian living in his kingdom, and that no mention be made of the West Bank. This incident says a lot about the political conditions in which the P.L.O. started out.

From the end of the 1950s onwards the Palestinian problem was at the forefront of Arab affairs. It came to prominence for a number of reasons: the growth of

revolutionary Arab nationalism, the failure of the 1955-56
secret negotiations between Israel and Egypt, an
increasingly hard line in Tel Aviv, and Israel's participation in the Anglo-French attack on Egypt. But Iraq, where
General Qassem had taken power, brought the issue up
again, and in spectacular fashion: in 1959 Baghdad
proposed the setting up of a Palestinian government in
Gaza and on the West Bank, and the proclamation of a
Palestinian Republic. In so doing Qassem was going
against Hussein, who had annexed the West Bank, as well
as the revolutionary Arab nationalists like Nasser and the
Baathists, who argued that the only solution to the
Palestinian problem lay in Arab unity. By the same token
he gave encouragement to the current of Palestinian
political opinion that favoured autonomy vis-a-vis the
Arab governments. Traces of his ideas can still be found in
Palestinian circles and undoubtedly influenced the Fatah
leaders. Despite Qassem's fall, in February 1963, the
problem of Palestine and its future remained on the
agenda. As we have seen it was Israel's decision that year to
divert the waters of the River Jordan which led the
January 1964 Arab Summit in Cairo to set up the P.L.O.

Although the Palestinian people were not completely
unaware of the movement's awakening, its foundation was
marked by inter-Arab rivalries and contradictions. The
inaugural congress which went on from 28 May to 2 June
1964, and was attended by 420 delegates, had to treat all
the Arab protagonists with care, and most especially King
Hussein and Nasser, who had a controlling hand in the
organisation. The resolutions which were adopted made
no reference to the sovereignty of the Palestinian people,
much less of some hypothetical state. Thus was the P.L.O.
born. Although it was a closely controlled organisation it
did nevertheless symbolise, even at this stage, the rebirth
of Palestinian nationalism and its forceful appearance on
the Middle Eastern chessboard.

1966-67: a crisis situation arose between Jordan and the
P.L.O.; the P.L.O. sided with Nasser against Hussein and
set about mobilising the Palestinian people. On 13
November 1966 an Israeli raid claimed 20 victims in the
village of Samoa, without any response from the

Jordanian army. This brought the Palestinian population on the West Bank, in Hebron, Ramallah, Tulkarem, Jericho and Jerusalem, out onto the streets. They demanded arms to defend themselves and clashed with Hashemite troops. The P.L.O. supported the demands made by the people on the West Bank, which led to a break with Amman. It was not until just before the Six Day War that relations were re-established. The P.L.O.'s adoption of this relatively combative stance was in part due to their not having a monopoly of representation in the Palestinian resistance: the Arab Nationalist Movement (A.N.M.) and Fatah provided strong competition.

For the A.N.M., as its name shows, Arab unity was the sum total of its strategy. Its origins went back to the war in Palestine, but it really began its development among a few intellectuals at the Arab University of Beirut in 1951. The A.N.M. had a presence in a number of Arab countries, and created a Palestinian section in 1964. It won substantial backing in the refugee camps in Lebanon, Syria and Gaza. As converts to Nasserism they were convinced that the only possible course for Palestinian national liberation lay in Arab unity; they therefore continually put themselves forward as far more active than the P.L.O. The leadership included George Habash and Wadi Hadad as well as a left-wing group centred around Nayef Hawatmeh and the Lebanese Mohsen Ibrahim.

Casting an eye over the list of the 420 delegates to the first Palestinian National Congress you find a number of previously unknown young men's names: Yasser Arafat, Khalil Wazir (Abu Jihad), Khaled Hassan and Kamal Adwan. They were members of a secret and mysterious organisation, Fatah, which had been set up in Kuwait in October 1959. Most of its leaders had received their political education in Cairo in the Palestinian Students' Union and had taken part in the fighting against the Israeli occupation of Gaza in 1956. Their policy stemmed from the impact of two main events: the break-up of the United Arab Republic in 1961 which effectively put an end to ideas of Arab unity as the precondition for the liberation of Palestine, and the victory of the Algerian revolution in 1962 which underlined the need to rely on their own forces and to develop the armed struggle. The logical corollary of this was their credo, that the liberation of Palestine would be achieved by the Palestinians themselves, and that the Arab states should 'keep their hands off' and stand back to watch while the Palestinians conducted their struggle against the Zionists.

The start of the armed struggle on 1 January 1965 acted as a magnet for Fatah. Before then they had had a limited impact, most Palestinian support going to either the A.N.M. or the P.L.O. This change is described by an A.N.M. leader: 'In 1964 a messenger from Fatah contacted us and proposed that our two organisations should co-ordinate action. We accepted, even though Fatah at that time had no presence at all among the people. We suggested reaching agreement on a political programme. The Fatah representative refused, asserting that for them unity was to be achieved through joint military action. The negotiations broke down. From 1965 onwards Fatah engaged in military action while we were telling our activists that we had to wait, to train and so on … So we saw our men going off and joining Al Fatah. The man we had met was called Yasser Arafat.'

The Time of the Fedayeen

The Six Day War marked the opening of a new era for the Palestinian nationalist movement. In the space of a few days everything in the Middle East was turned upside down. Nasserism in its earliest form was already on the wane; it now suffered a decisive blow. It became strikingly obvious that the Arabs were incapable of solving the Palestinian problem, while the P.L.O. and A.N.M. leaders linked to the Arab governments were also discredited. Israel's occupation of the West Bank, the Gaza Strip, Egyptian Sinai and the Syrian Golan Heights meant that Israelis and Palestinians were face to face with each other on a large scale for the first time since 1948. The Palestinian dimension of the Arab-Israeli conflict came to dominate everything else.

The Palestinian scene changed as events changed. Fatah-dominated Palestinian commando activity spread in

Jordan, while more and more incidents of armed resistance occurred in Gaza and on the West Bank. Crisis developed within the P.L.O. Shukeiri resigned at the end of 1967. In July 1968 the Palestine National Council, the P.L.O.'s highest body, held a meeting at which Al Fatah and other *fedayeen* representatives were present. They adopted a series of statutes and a new National Charter, which has now become extremely well known. A few months later the fifth National Council appointed Yasser Arafat as Chairman of the Executive Committee of the P.L.O. On 6 May 1970 a dozen Palestinian organisations came together in an agreement by which they all recognised the P.L.O. as the umbrella structure of Palestinian national unity. This was the beginning of the P.L.O. as we know it today.

This process of metamorphosis within the P.L.O. highlights two essential aspects of the organisation which set it apart from other national liberation movements: the proliferation of groups that go to make it up, and the autonomy each group has, so that they can make decisions which are at odds with the P.L.O. line. As well as Yasser Arafat's Fatah there is the Popular Front for the Liberation of Palestine (P.F.L.P.) led by George Habash, from which splits have created the P.F.L.P.-General Command, under Ahmed Jabril, and the Democratic Front for the Liberation of Palestine (D.F.L.P.), under Nayef Hawatmeh. Some Arab governments have created their own organisations in order to influence the P.L.O., for example the Syrian Baathist-inspired Saika and the Iraqi Baathist Arab Liberation Front (A.L.F.). In passing we should also note that there are several tiny groups that are more or less ephemeral. The new P.L.O. enjoyed support, to some degree, from a number of Arab leaders, but first and foremost from Nasser. Although it did not represent all the Palestinians it had great influence in the refugee camps in Jordan and Lebanon.

Armed struggle was a central theme for Al Fatah: for the new P.L.O. it was 'the only road leading to the liberation of Palestine'. After the failure of its attempt to establish itself on the West Bank at the end of 1967 the Palestinian resistance fell back on safe bases in Jordan and

then in Lebanon. The period from 1968-70 saw a steady
development of military operations which was symbolised
by the battle of Karameh, a little village a few kilometres
west of the River Jordan which the *fedayeen* used as a base.
The Defence forces attacked at dawn on 22 March 1968.
Several hundred men supported by armoured cars and
artillery crossed the river. Fighting went on all day. The
Israeli army withdrew in the evening after suffering heavy
losses in both men and materials. The prestige of the
fedayeen rocketed after fighting alongside the Jordanian
army in this battle. Thousands of Palestinians joined the
commandos.

But the high hopes that followed Karameh – hopes that
guerilla struggle would be irresistible and that the P.L.O.
would make military alliances with the Arab governments
– proved to be unfounded. Despite an increase in the
number of 'incidents' – from 97 in the second half of 1967
to 2,432 in 1969 – by 1970 the Israeli army had set up a
formidable system of crosschecking on the West Bank. A
very fine mesh net was put over the area making it
exceptionally difficult for the commandos to slip through
and operate effectively.

What was more worrying was the state of relations
between the P.L.O. and the Arab governments. The
new-style Palestinian resistance was receiving support
from Nasser. And in Cairo in November 1969 a series of
accords had been signed with the Lebanese government
officially sanctioning the P.L.O. presence in Lebanon. But
these achievements in themselves were not enough to
overcome the main contradiction that the P.L.O. has
always had to put up with: on the one hand victory is
impossible without Arab support, while on the other hand
the armed struggle serves only to antagonise those whose
support is needed. In Lebanon and Jordan where the
P.L.O. has a military presence it comes into conflict with
the central government. Through its influence over the
Palestinians the resistance movement either brings these
countries into conflict with Israel or draws Israeli reprisals
upon them. As far as the other countries are concerned
the Palestinian strategy, aiming at the total liberation of
Palestine, is incompatible with the short-term goals of

Egypt and Jordan, namely Israeli withdrawal solely from
the territories occupied in 1967.

The P.L.O. had rejected out of hand the U.N. Security
Council Resolution 242 of November 1967 which, though
guaranteeing Israel's right to live in peace, made no
mention of the national rights of the Palestinians, whom it
referred to as 'refugees'. The rejection had dramatic
repercussions, from as early as July 1970, when Nasser
and King Hussein accepted the initiative of the American
Secretary of State, the Rogers Plan. The resistance
attacked the American plan and by implication the
Egyptian leader, seriously underestimating the conster-
nation this would cause amongst the Palestinian masses for
whom Nasser was an idol. But most serious of all were the
events of September 1970 when the P.L.O. allowed itself
to be led by its left wing into a power struggle with the
Hashemite Kingdom. True, the Palestinian presence in
Jordan had sparked off conflicts with the Jordanian
authorities over the years, for example in November 1968,
February 1970 and July 1970. But this struggle took place
at a very ill chosen moment. The resistance movement was
isolated, cut off from its closest ally, Egypt. In Jordan it
was possible to say that they constituted a state within a
state, and their activities gave rise to strong hostility which
went far beyond leadership circles. The P.F.L.P. and
D.F.L.P. slogan 'All power to the resistance' made it all the
easier for them to be isolated. These were the conditions in
which the P.F.L.P. launched its attack on Hussein's
regime.

On 7 September 1970 P.F.L.P. commandos hijacked
three airliners, one belonging to the Israeli state airline, El
Al, one to Swissair and the third to T.W.A.; they took the
planes to the Jordanian town of Zarka. The airport was
proclaimed a Palestinian 'liberated zone'. Hundreds of
passengers were held as hostages. International opinion
was aroused and the Americans used the opportunity to
make a show of force in the Mediterranean. While this was
going on the adventurists of the P.F.L.P. targeted their
attacks on the King, declaring that 'Amman was blocking
the liberation of Palestine'. After many delays and
postponements, and despite the P.F.L.P. being suspended

from P.L.O. organisations at Yasser Arafat's request, the trap was closing. Hussein decided to deal with the whole resistance movement once and for all. On 16 September he set up a military government and ordered the army in. Fighting of appalling ferocity went on until the 27th.

Iraq, which had troops stationed in Jordan, and had promised to help the P.L.O., did not make a move. Syria began to intervene militarily, then withdrew; they were being threatened by Israel and the United States, and were paralysed by internal dissent: the Air Force Chief of Staff, a certain Hafez Assad, had refused to provide air cover for the Syrian armoured column's penetration into Jordan. Only Nasser tried to save the P.L.O., by getting Hussein and Arafat to sign agreements that brought an end to the slaughter. The Egyptian leader only lasted a few hours longer; he was struck down by a coronary. The agreements which were signed were favourable to the P.L.O., but they were never applied. The balance of power in Jordan had changed. Within a year the army were to expel all the *fedayeen* from the kingdom.

The resistance had lost its first major battle. Not against Israel but against an Arab country. There is a Palestinian saying, 'all the revolutions conceived in Palestine are aborted in Arab capitals'.

From Black September to the U.N.

After their expulsion from Jordan, the P.L.O. went through a lean period. Unable to endanger Israel militarily and with, as yet, too narrow a political base to fall back on, it faced the prospect of extinction. It was quite possible that it would disappear from the Middle Eastern political scene. At this point the Palestinians opted for international terrorism, symbolised at its most spectacular, and its bloodiest, by the Al Fatah creation known as the Black September organisation. One of the Fatah leaders, described Black September as an auxiliary at a time when the resistance was not able to fully carry out its military and political functions. He argued that the organisation expressed the Palestinians' deeply held feelings of frustration and indignation at the killings in Jordan and at the complicity that had made such things possible.

But frustration cannot take the place of policy. The results were less than convincing. The massacre of Israeli athletes at the Munich Olympics in 1972 did more than anything else to discredit the Palestinian movement and to identify it long-term with international terrorism. Yet at the same time the P.L.O. was laying the groundwork of a new type of activity. Increasingly attention was paid to diplomacy and to relations with progressive forces on an international scale, particularly with the socialist countries. Political work increased in scale, particularly in Gaza and on the West Bank. The ties that had been established in Jordan with the Lebanese national movement were forged into very close links. This gradual change in resistance practice influenced and transformed political thought.

Up until 1967 the P.L.O.'s objectives had dogmatic simplicity: the liberation of Palestine and its return to the Arab world. The first consequence of this was that the Israelis should go back to where they had come from – which is putting it in the mildest terms used at the time. No mention was made of the creation of a Palestinian state.

The Six Day War ended these certainties. Al Fatah put forward a new slogan 'A Democratic Palestinian State', which underlined the Palestinian desire for self-determination as well as acceptance that Jews, Christians and Muslims could coexist. Although it maintained the need to destroy the 'Zionist entity', Fatah now took into account the fact that there were hundreds of thousands of Jews in Palestine. If they so wished they could live in the new state. Unrealistic though it was, this did mark an important stage in the long drawn-out development of Palestinian policy.

The logical conclusions were drawn: at long last the existence of Israeli Jews had been recognised: why not establish a dialogue with them? This was how the first contacts were made between Israelis and Palestinians. But surely the idea of a single state was contradictory? If Israeli Jews were to remain in Palestine and enjoy the same rights as everyone else, how could they be omitted from the process of drawing up the statutes of the new state? What would happen if the majority of Israelis declined the invitation to live in the same state as the Palestinians? Did not accepting a Jewish presence imply the idea of Jewish self-determination? All of these doubts fuelled a nationalist trend opposed to the 'Democratic State' slogan. But this position was finally adopted by the P.L.O. in the aftermath of the Black September massacres in March 1971.

The National Charter must be mentioned, since it concerned the Jewish presence in Palestine. It had been adopted in July 1968 at a time when Fatah had yet to acquire a majority within the P.L.O. Article 6 states 'Jews who had normally resided in Palestine will be considered as Palestinians'. Since other Council documents make it clear that the 'Zionist invasion' dated from 1917, there were in fact hardly any Israeli Jews in 1968 who came into the category. Article 6 was viewed abroad as a reassertion of Shukeiri's mythical aim – to 'drive Israel into the sea', and enabled Israeli propaganda to make capital out of the situation. The Charter remains unchanged, despite a number of attempts to modify its contents and even though it contradicts the objects of subsequent P.L.O. campaigns. Indeed some elements within the resistance consider the Charter as a guarantee against Yasser Arafat's attempts to steer the P.L.O. in the direction of political solutions. The Charter does, after all, affirm the primacy of the armed struggle and the duty to liberate the whole of Palestine.

The ultimate paradox came at the sixteenth congress in Algiers in February 1983 which ratified the Fez Plan, guaranteeing peace for 'all the states in the area', but at the same time reaffirming the validity of the Charter. The apparent illogicality of the two statements is explained by the P.L.O. leadership's desire to preserve the movement's unity by maintaining a consensus between elements that from to time oppose each other. When asked about the Charter in Geneva in September 1983, Arafat felt able to joke about it: 'You know, the Charter is like the Talmud for us ... Let's talk about P.L.O. policies instead'. But Arafat's irony does not make up for the harm caused by the Charter to the people who wrote it.

There was no chance at all of beginning to implement

the Democratic State plan, let alone the National Charter. This was all the more damaging in the period after 1972-3 when, despite its defeat in Jordan, the P.L.O. became a key factor in the Middle East equation. The Black September massacres had disgusted the West Bank Palestinians so much that they repudiated their allegiance to the Hashemite Kingdom. Their national consciousness rose, and in August 1973, when the Palestine National Front in the occupied territories was created and claimed to be part of the P.L.O., it won support from the people in Gaza and on the West Bank. This was also the time when the P.L.O. received international recognition. The October 1973 war posed a dilemma to the resistance by opening the way to a global settlement of the problem. Refusing such a settlement meant risking confrontation not just with Israel but also with Egypt and Syria, its closest allies among the Arab states. What mattered more was allowing King Hussein to negotiate the future of the West Bank with Israel on his own. The other alternative was for the P.L.O. to accept the difficult task of becoming involved in the peace process, which meant that it had to compromise. There was hesitation and ambiguity before the majority of the resistance opted for the latter alternative.

In June 1974 the 12th Palestinian National Congress opened after months of bitter debate. A resolution was adopted stating that the P.L.O. would struggle to 'establish the people's independent and fighting sovereignty in every part of Palestinian land to be liberated'. This was the first time that the resistance had accepted an intermediate goal, or anything other than the liberation of all of Palestine. This was still mentioned as the long term objective, for fear of a split, but the P.L.O. leadership now had some room for manoeuvre which made it possible for them to get involved in the peace process. This soon produced results: in October 1974 the Arab League recognised the P.L.O. as 'the sole representative of the Palestinian people'. A month later Yasser Arafat received a triumphal welcome at the U.N. General Assembly. The P.L.O. had achieved international recognition as a reward for ten years hard work.

Internal Divisions

Internal rumblings accompanied the P.L.O.'s steady advance. Two tendencies confronted each other after the twelfth Palestinian National Council: they became known as the 'realists' and the 'rejectionists'.

The realists included Arafat, and the core of Fatah, and had the support of the Communists and the D.F.L.P. as well as that of a 'moderate', right wing group which favoured compromise with the Americans on any terms. Its roots were chiefly in the occupied territories where the Arab population were deeply disturbed by Israeli colonisation and annexation. Their position in the refugee camps, however, was more tenuous. The 'refugees' from towns and villages within the frontiers of Israel were unwilling to give up the idea of returning to their homes. From its hegemonic position in the camps Fatah undertook activity from 1972 onwards which gradually overcame this reluctance.

The rejectionist front was also heterogeneous. It brought together the P.F.L.P., led by George Habash, and a number of small pro-Iraqi and pro-Libyan organisations. Some Fatah elements were also sympathetic to it and, like Abud Nidal, broke with Arafat, while others like Abu Salah and Abu Musa remained within Fatah. Support also came from ultra right wing nationalist groups. The front's social base was both among the refugees in the camps, and among the rich Palestinian diaspora living in the Persian Gulf. Abu Iyad criticised these latter supporters, arguing that they could afford the luxury of intransigence since they had no fear of eternal exile. Very nearly the same could be said of some of the P.L.O. bureaucrats sitting in comfort in Beirut.

The history of the P.L.O. from 1973 to today has been marked by clashes and conflicts between these two shifting tendencies. They have not prevented the leadership of the P.L.O. from working to impose a diplomatic solution, for example in demanding the participation of the Palestinian Resistance in an international conference on the Middle East. But these diplomatic initiatives became bogged down in the development of the Lebanese crisis. From 1972-73 onwards the P.L.O. has been part of the Lebanese imbroglio. Although the P.L.O. is not responsible for all the conflicts which are tearing the country apart – far from it – the Palestinian presence in the country and the activities of the resistance have made matters worse. Following the outbreak of civil war in April 1975 the leadership of Al Fatah, realising the regional and international implications involved, did everything it could to keep out of the conflict. But they failed to do so; the trap could not be avoided. There was no room for onlookers in Lebanon. From the first half of 1976 the P.L.O. and its left wing Lebanese allies were in the driving seat. Victory seemed within their grasp; to such an extent that Lebanon's neighbours began to fear a left wing take over of power in Beirut. Tel Aviv increased its support to the Phalangists, and on 1 June 1976 the Syrian Army crossed the border.

This operation had received the go-ahead from Israel and also from the United States, with whom Damascus had been discreetly negotiating for some months. Relations between Nixon and Assad were better than ever. The P.L.O. and their allies were crushed by the Syrian army and were only saved *in extremis* by an inter-Arab agreement. At the end of 1976 there was a 'hot' peace in Lebanon. The Camp David accords certainly led to an upset in the alliances between Damascus and Lebanon, but the mistrust caused by the bloody events of 1976 – the Palestinians will never forget, and rightly so, the massacres in the Tal el Zaatar camp – created a deep rift between Arafat and Hafez el Assad.

Despite these setbacks in Lebanon, the P.L.O. reaffirmed its commitment to negotiation at the thirteenth Palestine National Council meeting in Cairo in March 1977. The final resolution refers to the idea of an independent Palestinian state, stresses the Palestinian wish to take part in an international conference and advocates dialogue with those Israeli forces 'struggling against the theory and practice of Zionism'. This represented a defeat for the rejectionists and some of them rejoined the leadership of the P.L.O.

The future seemed almost rosy: the newly elected

President Carter referred to the Palestinians' right to a homeland for the first time. But changes come thick and fast in the Middle East. Menachem Begin's victory in the Israeli general election in 1977, followed by Anwar Sadat's visit to Jerusalem, pushed the P.L.O. onto the sidelines and put back a global settlement once again.

The Palestinian Diaspora

Israel	555,000
West Bank	830,000
Gaza Strip	450,000
Jordan	1,150,000
Syria	220,000
Lebanon	370,000
Kuwait	300,000
Saudi Arabia	140,000
Other Gulf States including	
Iraq and Oman	130,000
Egypt	45,000
Libya	25,000
United States	100,000
Other countries	140,000
Total	4,450,000

These figures are based on the estimates of the P.L.O. Central Statistical Bureau, for 1981. In some cases these may be over-estimates, although the figures for Israel, the West Bank and Gaza are correct.

Palestinians in Israel

Just who are these Palestinians that we are talking about? There are more than four million of them scattered throughout the world. They have had extremely diverse social and political experiences and live in very varied conditions. They comprise three main groups: those who live in the historic lands of Palestine (Israel, the West Bank and Gaza), those in Jordan, and finally those who have settled for one reason or another in the other Arab countries. Among them there are nearly two million refugees. In 1948 and 1967 many fled and ended up in camps on the West Bank and in Gaza, Jordan, Syria and

Lebanon. Today they number more than 700,000.

The Palestinians in Israel are the Arabs who did not flee in the enforced exodus in 1948-9; at that time they numbered 160,000 and by 1983 there were nearly 700,000, or approximately 16.5% of the population of Israel. They are chiefly concentrated in three areas: Galilee in the north with Nazareth as its centre, a large triangle around Oum El Fahm, and a small triangle around the town of Tayiba. The U.N. partition plan had allocated these areas to the Arab state but Israel annexed them in 1949, and consequently considers their population as Israeli citizens – but only 'second zone' citizens. Until 1966 the Arabs in Israel lived under a military administration which imposed travel permits, a curfew and house arrest, and above all 'legalised' Israeli confiscation of Arab lands. In the name of exceptional measures systematic looting took place, for the benefit of the Jewish colonists.

Oum El Fahm was a fair-sized place in 1948 with a population of 6,500. Today it has some 20,000. This is how the inhabitants tell their story: 'We had corn, hay, everything in the valley ... all they have left us is the stony ground'. The commune which comprised 145,000 dunams (a dunam = 0.10 hectares) now comprises 20,000: 5,000 for housing and 15,000 full of stones. According to one villager quoted in the *Franco-Palestinian Friendship Bulletin* 'Each day the population rises and the land gets smaller'. He goes on to say, 'I want to extend my house. My brother is abroad. The government offers to sell me the few metres of land I need in exchange for the whole of his land. We have to give up 30 dunams of farmland in exchange for one dunam of land in the village'. According to the Committee for the Defense of Arab Land, the Israeli Government has confiscated 3,200,000 of the 4,000,000 dunams of land belonging to the Palestinians in 1948. Of the 800,000 which remain only 300,000 are cultivatable.

The structure of the Arab population has been turned upside down by these expropriations. At the beginning of the 1960s the population was 75% rural. Today the majority live in towns. 50% of the workforce engaged in industry and construction is Palestinian. These great changes produced, through complex processes, a heightened class consciousness. The Communist Party of Israel has become the expression of this consciousness and the voice of a national minority fighting for recognition of their rights. Between 40% and 50% of the Arab population vote for Communist candidates in elections. Succeeding Israeli governments have had some success in responding to this situation by playing on anti-communist feelings and highlighting the differences within the Arab community, whilst at the same time maintaining their policies of racial discrimination. 10% of the Palestinians are Druze. They alone are obliged to do military service; the government tries to set them at odds with their Muslim and Christian compatriots. (13% of the Palestinians in Israel are Christians.) In the same vein the different Zionist parties buy the support of the traditional leaders in order to obtain votes. The outcome of this is that some Arab villages vote for the Likud, some vote Labour, while others vote for the Jewish religious parties and even for the extreme right! These achievements notwithstanding, Israel's main weapon is continual repression. It reached its peak on 30 March 1976, 'Land Day', when the Israeli Army killed six and wounded dozens of Palestinians for demonstrating against the theft of their lands in Israel.

Like all Palestinians, the Arabs in Israel have invested heavily in education. Almost a third of the population, whose average age is very low, is at school. Hundreds of young intellectuals are produced every year. A cultural and national renaissance is taking place, thanks in part to the Arab press (*Al Itihad, Al Jadid*) and also to leading intellectuals such as Emile Habibi, Emile Tuma and Tawfik Zayad, the Communist Mayor of Nazareth, to name but a few.

Life Under Occupation

More than 800,000 Palestinians live on the West Bank and in East Jerusalem. 300,000 are refugees, a third of them in camps and the rest integrated into the community. The

West Bank is quite a wealthy area, with towns such as
Nablus, Ramallah and Hebron, not to mention the Arab
part of Jerusalem, all showing signs of prosperity.

In the early days of the 1967 war, the Israeli army used
the tried and trusty old methods of 1948: any tactic at all
so long as it drove the inhabitants towards Jordan. A
Palestinian from Tulkarem, a town in the North East,
describes what happened: 'Everyone in Tulkarem was
driven out. Not one of us was allowed to stay. My wife's
uncle was killed because he refused to leave. People took
clothes, money and gold and began to head east. Two days
later a rumour went round that we could go back. Many of
the villages around Tulkarem were also ordered to go
east'.

The result of this was 250,000 more refugees in Jordan,
whom the Israeli authorities would not allow to return to
their villages. U.N. pressure only succeeded in forcing
Israel to grant 20,000 permits, mostly to prominent and
wealthy people.

Israeli occupation is not like other kinds of occupation.
Most of the leaders in Tel Aviv believe that the West Bank
is an integral part of Eretz Israel, the land of Israel. They
dredge up its biblical names, Judea and Samaria. The
Palestinians are thus no more than intruders who, at best
can hope for the concession of some kind of autonomous
status. The true nature of Israel's conquest – for that is
what it is – can be seen daily in the ever-increasing number
of colonies, the confiscation of land, and the annexation of
Jerusalem. The colonisation programme was launched by
the Labour government. When it fell, in 1977, fifty-odd
colonies had been established, each consisting of between
3,500 and 4,000 inhabitants, as well as the 45,000-50,000
in the Jerusalem area. These new colonists, unlike their
predecessors of the 1920s and 30s, had little ideological or
religious motivation. Only a very few fanatics hid in
fortress-like camps and undertook no economic activity at
all. By contrast, Jerusalem and the surrounding district
attracted Israelis for purely material reasons: they could
find nowhere else to live.

This degeneration of Zionism did not stop the Labour
government's confiscation of land, or control of water

resources. And this policy was accompanied by the
economic integration of the West Bank into Israel. The
occupied territories were transformed into an important
market for Israeli exports. At the same time tens of
thousands of Palestinians moved in the other direction
every day to sell their labour at very low prices. In 1968
there were 5,000, in 1971 25,000 in 1979 40,000, and
these figures do not include the illegal workers, and
children in particular. Although the West Bank economy
prospers from the effects of their wages it is a false
prosperity: the Palestinian workers are strengthening
Israel, not the economy of their own country, which
remains stagnant.

But there is one aspect of this exploitation which is in
many ways positive: the growth of a Palestinian working
class which is bigger and more class conscious than in any
other Arab country. The industrial working class today
makes up 40% of the working population, while the
agricultural sector now employs only 25%. This transformation is hastening the gradual disappearance of
traditional society. Moral values and lifestyles are
changing. Relations based on traditional patronage and
custom are being worn away. The increasing fall in the
average age and the high level of education are
accentuating this process. One third of the population is
studying in some form, and every year 10,000 young
people finish secondary school. The young people in
secondary schools are in the forefront of resistance to the
occupation. The appearance of a new, more nationalist
intellectual elite has reduced the influence of the
traditional leaders and contributed greatly to the P.L.O.'s
success in establishing itself.

Following the rout of October 1967 the vast majority of
the West Bank population, including the establishment,
sought a return to the status quo, with the borders as they
had been on 4 June 1967. Twenty years of Hashemite
domination and enforced assimilation had expunged the
idea of a Palestinian national entity from the popular
consciousness. But a number of elements were to cause a
resurgence of nationalist feeling: prolonged subjugation,
struggles against colonisation, the Black September

massacres which served to discredit King Hussein, renewed contact with the Palestinians in Israel, the social changes described above and so on. Although the P.L.O. was unable to establish the armed struggle on the West Bank in the period 1967-70 it did begin to build up a good deal of support. The work done by Communist activists, who knew how to wage a political struggle and were experienced in clandestine methods, facilitated this process, which culminated in August 1973 in the creation of the Palestine National Front. Within a few months this wide-ranging grouping acquired a hegemonic position. So overwhelming was their influence that in the 1976 municipal elections candidates supported by the Front and the P.L.O. won over 80% of the seats and took control of the main towns on the West Bank. For the next few years these local administrations were to be decisive strongholds in the confrontation with the foreign presence.

The Gaza Strip

The Gaza Strip, which has been under Israeli occupation since 1967, is very much a different world. From 1949 onwards it remained under Egyptian administration. It is a poor and overpopulated strip of land. Three quarters of the people there are refugees. 200,000 of the 450,000 Palestinians in Gaza live crowded together in camps. Even the most superficial visitor is struck by the misery and despair that prevail. The 1967 Israeli conquest had the same results here as on the West Bank: the establishment of Jewish colonies and integration of the area into the Israeli economy. More than half the Palestinian workforce are employed in Israel. The average age is very low, and there is a high educational level, thanks to U.N. help for the Palestinian refugees. But there is no work, so the qualified people emigrate. This tendency can also be seen on the West Bank but in Gaza it attains alarming proportions.

Gaza, unlike the West Bank, witnessed an intense armed struggle between 1967 and 1971. The resolve of the Palestinians living there had been strengthened by their first experience of Israeli occupation in 1956-57. They were ardent nationalists. Most of the Al Fatah leaders grew up there. After the Six Day War they threw themselves headlong into guerilla warfare. General Sharon put an exceptionally brutal end to their campaign in 1971. But that did not mean the end of the resistance. From the beginning of the 1970s onwards they began to work more closely with the Palestinians on the West Bank, and to give increasing support to the P.L.O. The authorities tried to eradicate them in two ways: by using the hostility of Muslim integrationists towards the P.L.O., and by relentless repression.

A Palestinian lawyer describes what happened. 'All defendants appear in the dock before military tribunals with confessions already signed during investigation. They have to sign confessions written in Hebrew. A man under arrest is cut off from his family and his lawyer for weeks at a time and after interrogation is ready to sign anything at all. My clients have told me of the treatment they have received: beatings, being made to stand for long periods with their hands in the air, insults, threats, and so on.'

These are everyday occurrences in the occupied territories; a number of commissions of enquiry have confirmed that torture is used. The West Bank and Gaza also hold another miserable record: that of the highest number of political prisoners. Some of the youngest prisoners are adolescents. The emergency laws under which they are arrested date back to the time of the British mandate. As a result of these measures the Palestinians can stay in prison for years without trial: it is called 'preventive' or 'adminstrative' detention. Listing the human rights violations undergone by the Palestinians would fill a whole book.

The Palestinian Diaspora

There are just over a million Palestinians in Jordan. The figures are not very reliable. There is no distinction in Jordanian statistics between Palestinians and other citizens holding Jordanian passports. The only accurate figures are the U.N.W.R.A. statistics relating to refugees: more than 700,000, of whom 300,000 came from the West Bank and Gaza after 1967; of these some 200,000 live in camps.

The P.L.O. and Al Fatah's strongest support came from inside the camps until 1971. Following Black September all Palestinian activity was forbidden. The recent rapprochement between the P.L.O. and King Hussein has not yet led to this ban being lifted.

By way of conclusion to this brief survey some information is needed relating to the Palestinians in Lebanon, Syria, and the Gulf. In Lebanon Palestinian economic, social and political life was closely tied to the presence of the P.L.O. Through a variety of mass organisations (women's and young people's organisations, the Red Crescent, trade unions and self-help groups), the resistance was present among people in the camps. P.L.O. fighters and personnel necessary for the organisation's state-like bureaucratic apparatus, as well as workers for the industries they set up, all came from the camps. For these people who had experienced exodus more than once, and had then undergone Israeli reprisal raids, the P.L.O. meant everything. The P.L.O.'s departure from Beirut and then from Tripoli left the people behind in acute distress, leaderless and unprotected. The civil war which had destroyed much of the Lebanese state apparatus means that it is impossible to evaluate the plight in which this section of the Palestinian diaspora finds itself at the moment. But what happened at Sabra and Shatila is enough to indicate the extreme vulnerability of the Palestinians in Lebanon.

There are 200,000 Palestinians in Syria, all of them refugees. Almost 30% of them live in camps under strict political control which is not helped by the tense relations between the P.L.O. and the Damascus government. This is borne out by the ferocious manner in which pro-Arafat demonstrations during the siege of Tripoli were repressed.

Lastly, there are more than 600,000 Palestinians in the Gulf, more than half of them in Kuwait. They are recent immigrants, most of them arriving in the 1960s. At first the men came alone, then the families. While retaining their Palestinian character they have settled into the

community and are often to be found playing a role in the
economy of the Gulf States. There are Palestinians in
prominent positions, working as engineers, technicians,
skilled tradespeople, doctors, teachers, entrepreneurs and
journalists. In some places, such as Kuwait, they play a
significant political role as well, which is not unrelated to
the support the P.L.O. receives from most of the Gulf
States. The Gulf exiles are a small but influential
Palestinian minority. Their communities are rich and
strongly nationalist; they send substantial funds back to
their families as well as providing financial help for the
P.L.O.

Despite the sometimes deep differences between one
community and another there remain characteristics
which are shared by all Palestinians. Two in particular
stand out: on the one hand the very high educational level
which has no parallel in the Arab world and is comparable
with that of Israel, and on the other hand the development
of a working class which, though fragmented, has
continued to grow in both size and consciousness for more
than a decade and has achieved a strength unknown
elsewhere in the Islamic world.

The great achievement of the P.L.O. has been to build
on these solid foundations and to unite the vast majority of
Palestinians, regardless of frontiers and the changing
fortunes of struggle. Nothing has proved stronger than
the deeply-held feeling that they all – or almost all – share
that they are one people, with the same history and
culture, symbolised by poets such as Mahmoud Darwish or
writers such as Ghassan Khanafani.

How does the P.L.O. work?

The P.L.O. is first and foremost the Palestine National
Council which is both a parliament and a congress. It now
has more than 300 members and meets, in principle, every
year, although its meetings tend in practice to be more
spread out than that. One third of the members represent
organisations such as Fatah and the P.F.L.P. The other
two thirds represent 'mass organisations' (students, trade

unionists, women, sportspeople, writers and so on), independent personalities and delegates from the different communities in exile. Since 1981 one of the delegates to the P.N.C. has been representing Palestinians in Brazil! Over and above these 300-odd members there are a further 120 unnamed members who are the representatives from the West Bank and Gaza. However they are unable to attend the meetings because the Israeli authorities forbid all contact with the P.L.O. They are sorely missed. The West Bank and Gaza Palestinians are in the forefront of the resistance and more concerned than anyone else by its future course, yet although they should be playing a decisive role, they are unable to have any direct influence on P.L.O. decisions. One of the original features of the Palestinian Parliament is that it brings together all sorts of political tendencies and ideologies, from the Communists to the far right. Its debates are always lively and many views are expressed, particularly since the P.L.O. changed its tactics in 1973. Few liberation movements can pride themselves on such democratic debate encompassing such a wide range of opinions.

As early as 1970 Yasser Afafat explained why Fatah, which at that time had a position of hegemony within the P.L.O., did not intend to use force to resolve differences of opinion with other groups. 'Firstly', he argued, 'because fundamentally we do not believe in this way of doing things. Secondly, these organisations and their conflicts are an integral part of the contradictions of the Arab nation and who are we if we aren't part of that nation? Thirdly, because some of these groups are linked to Arab countries and any military confrontation with them would mean military confrontation with that country'.

But this great diversity of views also has a negative side. P.L.O. unity becomes an aim in itself. Consensus between all the tendencies is seen as the only way of coping with the complex situation the P.L.O. exists within, and as the best way of stopping the Arab countries from manipulating rivalry between the different Palestinian groups. The effect of this is that any little organisation at all can block P.L.O. decisions. Many observers see this as the cause of the P.L.O.'s persistently vague political line. Decisions taken by the P.N.C. are open to different, even widely divergent, interpretations. It is undoubtedly the case that the total intransigence of Israel's leaders and their rejection of all offers of negotiation, whether made in public or in secret, has not encouraged the P.L.O. to take a more clear-cut stance. But it must be said that the Palestinian leaders are aware that the experience of the last ten years, the tragic events in Beirut and their dramatic sequel in Tripoli, do put a question mark over this way of operating. The P.N.C. elects an Executive Committee of 15 members. It is composed of representatives of all the large organisations together with a number of independents. The President of the Executive Committee since 1969 has been Yasser Arafat, whose authority was never questioned before the sixteenth P.N.C. meeting in Algiers.

There is a Central Council between the legislative body (the P.N.C.) and the executive body (the E.C.) as well as a whole series of institutions and mass organisations: the Palestinian Red Cross, the information department issuing publications, the Wafa press agency, the education department running schools, and with tens of thousands of students studying in universities throughout the world; the political department which is really the Ministry of Foreign Affairs with more than a hundred diplomatic representatives abroad; research, statistical and planning centres; the Palestine National Fund, which is the Ministry of Finance, in control of the considerable revenues coming from Arab aid as well a tax levied on the Palestinians. Within the occupied territories there are the local administrations which have not been removed by the occupying power, charitable and social organisations and trades unions. To sum up, the P.L.O. has an organisation very similar to that of a state. Because they were mainly centred on Beirut, the 1982 war in Lebanon did considerable harm to these organisations. At the present time the P.L.O. is encountering innumerable obstacles caused by being scattered, and by uncertainty about what is going to happen next.

From Autonomy to Annexation

On 19 November 1977 President Sadat went to Jerusalem. This historic event was analysed in the first part of the book; at this point we should note the Palestinian reaction to it. After some hesitation the P.L.O. condemned the visit for several reasons. Sadat went to Israel without any reference to other Arab leaders. In so doing he *de facto* recognised the Israeli state without any reciprocal gesture from Israel. In addition, and most importantly, it put an end to the Geneva Conference that the United States and the Soviet Union had agreed to recall and which the P.L.O. supported. In the event P.L.O. fears proved justified: after Jerusalem Sadat went to Camp David.

As we saw earlier, the accords reached at Camp David were in two parts, the second part dealing with the West Bank and Gaza. From its strong position the Israeli Government was able to use the ambiguity of the text to avoid making any concessions on this question.

Just what did the documents signed by Carter, Begin and Sadat mean? They provided for 'the full autonomy of the inhabitants' during a five year transition period. Furthermore 'the Israeli military government and its civilian adminstration will be withdrawn as soon as a self-governing authority has been freely elected by the inhabitants of these areas'. To achieve this end, 'Egypt, Israel and Jordan will agree on the modalities for establishing the elected self-governing authorities'. Palestinians from the West Bank and Gaza could be included in the Egyptian or Jordanian delegations, providing that all parties (including Israel) agreed. After the election some Israeli forces would be withdrawn and others redeployed.

Finally in the first three years of the transition period (that is to say after the election of the autonomous authority) the future of the territories would be decided by negotiation. The settlement would take into consideration 'the legitimate rights of the Palestinian people and their just requirements'. In a letter to Menachem Begin attached to the treaty by way of clarification Jimmy Carter spelled out that he had been informed that wherever the treaty mentioned 'Palestinians' or 'Palestinian people' the

Israeli Premier understood 'Palestinian Arabs', and that wherever it mentioned 'The West Bank' he understood 'Judea and Samaria'.

There was no answer to a number of key questions: the problem of refugees, whose return was subject to Israeli agreement, the status of Jerusalem, the role of Jordan, which had not been consulted, and so on. But above all, the question of a Palestinian state remained suspended in the air: could the promised autonomy lead to self determination, as some analysts claimed at the time? The texts are certainly vague and open to differing interpretations. But the position of the Begin government was crystal clear. The Likud announced that at the end of the five year transition period it would claim sovereignty over the West Bank and Gaza. It rejected the idea of a return to pre-1967 frontiers, refused to hand back Arab Jerusalem and dismissed any idea of a Palestinian state.

As for the freeze on Jewish settlements in 'Judea and Samaria', which Camp David stipulated, Begin completely disregarded this part of the accord. They began again on a large scale in 1979. Egypt, paralysed while awaiting the 'liberation' of Sinai, neither could nor would take action to stop it. All the Israelis had to do was to stick to their conception of 'autonomy': the state of Israel would have responsibility for internal security, all the lands of the great estates and water distribution; the settlers and settlements were to be answerable only to the Israeli state; it would also control the postal and telecommunications services, exports and imports, travel to Arab countries, transfers of capital, and so on. Given this state of affairs nobody was surprised at the failure of the Israeli-Egyptian 'autonomy' negotiations.

The most clear-cut opposition to the accords, came from the population of the West Bank and Gaza. When they were announced in September 1978 they were met by insurrection. On 1 October 150 prominent figures and political representatives from the West Bank held a national conference to deliver to Carter, Begin and Sadat a categorical reply: outright rejection and formal condemnation of the Camp David accords. A similar congress took place in Gaza on 20 October and showed the same determination: 'No to autonomy, yes to the P.L.O.'. In March 1979 the signing of the peace treaty between Israel and Egypt sparked off another insurrection. There could no longer be any doubt about the feelings of the Palestinians in the 'interior'.

The P.L.O. also categorically rejected the accords. The Arab heads of state, meeting in Baghdad in November 1978, did however shift their traditional position significantly. While expressing their hostility to Camp David the Arab leaders adopted a realistic view. Although they demanded the evacuation of the territories occupied in 1967, including East Jerusalem, and the right of the Palestinians to a state of their own, they did *de facto* accept the existence of Israel. They reaffirmed that the P.L.O. was the only legitimate representative of the Palestinian people. Considerable financial assistance was made available, intended for the Palestinians and the 'front line states'. The Baghdad meeting also finally ratified the break with Egypt which had taken place after the Israeli-Egyptian peace treaty. What was most important of all for Yasser Arafat was the extent of support for moves towards reconciliation between Damascus and Baghdad, which was to prove short-lived, and the beginning of a rapprochement between the P.L.O. and Jordan.

The Baghdad meeting was a great boost for the P.L.O.: Arafat visited Vienna, Ankara, Madrid, Lisbon, New Delhi and Tokyo. Time and again he called for negotiations. He approved the secret discussions that had been taking place between the P.L.O. and peace-seeking elements within Israel since 1976. These discussions had included numerous meetings in Paris between Issam Sartawi of the P.N.C. and General Peled. And the discussions continued, in spite of Palestinian extremists like the Abu Nidal groups, and the Israeli secret services, who repeatedly made attempts on the lives of those who were trying to create a dialogue, and on the most realistic elements within the P.L.O.: Hammami, Kalak, Khader, Henri Curiel and others.

But there can be no doubt that the P.L.O. has lost the political initiative. Increasing isolation seems to have no effect on Tel Aviv. The Israeli leaders are convinced that they have a great advantage in the peace with Egypt, and are confident of total American backing, especially since the development of a directly interventionist Middle East strategy which the United States has been pursuing since the fall of the Shah. As a result they have continued to adopt the same reckless approach that we described in the first chapter of this book. In the occupied territories this approach takes the form of the destruction of local government, bloody attacks aided by settlers and Arab 'collaborators' from the 'Village League', and above all the stepping up of colonisation. Because of a shortage of 'pioneers' eager to go to the occupied territories, the government offers homes or council flats in the towns on very favourable terms to attract low income Israelis, most of whom are Oriental Jews. Road improvements and the short distances involved mean that it is easy to travel from home to work. The aim is to settle 100,000 more Israelis in the coming years; the Begin government was very well aware that it was engaged in a race against time.

Where next after Beirut, Tripoli and Amman?

Israeli extremism culminated in the invasion of Lebanon. After three dramatic and bloody months the P.L.O. were forced out of Beirut. It seemed that a moral victory made up for their military defeat. There seemed to be new possibilities in the offing. In a speech on 1 September 1982 Ronald Reagan put forward a new peace plan. Eight days later, at the end of the Fez summit, the Arab states published their own plan. Arafat and King Hussein began discussions with a view to defining a 'Palestine-Jordan confederation', which would somehow equate demands for an independent Palestinian state with American insistence on 'association with Jordan'.

Any progress was blocked by Israeli and American intransigence in rejecting P.L.O. participation in the peace progress. The crisis within the P.L.O. which had been simmering ever since their departure from Beirut now boiled over into the open. This new exodus had had profound effects: the Palestinian resistance had lost the state-like structures it had created in Lebanon. It was severely weakened militarily. Its command structures and cadres were scattered in a dozen different countries. It was cut off from its roots in the Palestinian masses, where it had maintained a physical presence. For the first time since 1967 the P.L.O. had no base and was out of the front line. The malaise this caused prompted questions about both the movement's strategy and the way it operated.

On top of this came a crisis in relations with Damascus. President Assad decided to 'control' the Palestinians, first by encouraging mutiny within the P.L.O. and, after this failed, by allowing his tanks to be used to expel the Palestinians from the Bekaa Valley. His forces then besieged Tripoli where Arafat had sought refuge. However Palestinians everywhere showed their trust in their leader, and by so doing symbolised their unity. Helped by international concern about their plight, the P.L.O. were able to evacuate their fighters (fedayin) from Tripoli at the end of 1983. This marked the end of the Lebanese chapter in P.L.O. history, which had begun back in 1968. It was a bloody end: the massacres carried out by the Amal militia in the spring of 1984, emulating the horrific bloodbath perpetrated by the Phalangists with the complicity of the Israeli Army in September 1982, seemed to be a symbol for the end of an epoch.

At this juncture Yasser Arafat decided to force the issue. In December 1983, looking to Cairo to counter Syrian hegemony, he met and sought reconciliation with the Egyptian President Hosni Mubarak. In November 1984, backed almost solely by Fatah, he summoned the 17th Palestinian National Council to meet in Amman. Although the meeting was quorate, the rift between Al Fatah and the other groups within the P.L.O. grew wider still. Finally, in February 1985 he signed an agreement with King Hussein which provided for setting up a joint Palestinian-Jordanian delegation to begin peace negotiations. But all these endeavours and concessions have yet to achieve a real breakthrough towards peace. Neither Washington nor Tel Aviv seem ready to make any concessions.

For the P.L.O. leader the situation is all the more worrying because these policies have proved costly. Relations between the P.L.O. and the U.S.S.R. are

strained. He faces twofold opposition within the P.L.O.:
from the National Safety Front, made up of small
pro-Syrian groups supported by the P.F.L.P., and from
the D.F.L.P. and the C.P.P. The Palestinians in the
occupied territories and in exile are very much in disarray.
What should the P.L.O.'s political strategy be now? How
should the resistance be organised? Five years after
leaving Beirut these questions remain unanswered.

Chapter Four

Lebanon: A Festering Sore

Lebanon, a little country on the Eastern shores of the Mediterranean, has one of the highest population density figures in the Middle East. At the outbreak of the civil war the population was estimated at 3,000,000. Today, as a result of casualties and emigration, it has fallen to something in the region of 2,500,000. The country is marked by two demographic features which have political implications.

Firstly, there is a large foreign population: 300,000-400,000 Palestinians, plus 500,000 Syrians (according to 1975 figures) working in agriculture and industry. Secondly there is the phenomenon of emigration. There are Lebanese all over the world. To begin with only Christians left, but for some time now emigration has spread to include Muslims. The Lebanese wield considerable economic weight in the Gulf. Some have settled in the United States, others in Latin America or in Africa. Are these emigrants, who for the most part are Christians, still Lebanese citizens? This is anything but an academic question in a country where a balance between the different communities seems to be the key to stability.

A Guide to the Lebanon

To an untrained eye, or to a complete stranger, at first sight Lebanon looks like a collection of different religious groups: there are 17 in all. Life in the country has been governed by relations between them since independence. Some people have even referred to the present events as

'Wars of Religion'. To understand this tiny country we need to examine this amalgam of sects and splinter groups.

The Druze

Although not very strong in numbers the Druze are a separate community in Lebanon, both doctrinally and because of their decisive role in the creation of modern Lebanon. The sect comes from one of the branches of Shiism, with origins going back to a Fatimid Caliphate in Cairo in the tenth century.

Caliph Al Hakim, who ruled from 996-1021 sought recognition as the divine 'Seventh Imam' of Shiite tradition. After his death, which may have been murder, his supporters were persecuted. His former Vizir, Al Daruzi, took refuge in Syria where he succeeded in converting the southern tribes to belief in his master's divinity. The sect owes its name to him. A few years later, in 1043, they stopped preaching the new faith. The Druze community was 'closed'. Proselytism and conversion were forbidden. 'The veil is drawn, the door closed, the ink dry and the pen broken'. The doctrine they created was esoteric, the preserve of a tiny cast of wise men largely influenced by Aristotelian and Neo-Platonic Greek philosophy. So different are they that other Muslims consider them as apostates.

The first Druze Emirate dates back to the twelfth century. Even at that stage it was situated in the central area of Mount Lebanon around Cherif, Gharb and Metn which is still its territorial base today. With the accession of the Maan dynasty in the 16th century the great Druze era began. It culminated in the reign of Fakhreddin II who is generally held to be one of the founders of modern Lebanon. He was certainly the first chief to unify the territories which now make up the country. He even challenged the authority of his suzerain, the Ottoman Caliph, who eventually had him executed after a long struggle. Fakhreddin did not hesitate to form alliances with Christians in his fight against the Turks, notably with the Duke of Tuscany. He was even party to spreading in

Europe the legend that the Druze were descended from Crusaders and that their name came from the French town of Dreux!

Fakhreddin's reign was one of the rare periods of unification that Lebanon has known up to the present day. The other was just before the modern period and occurred under the rule of Bashir II, known as Bashir the Great, who ruled from 1788 to 1840. Bashir came from the influential Shebab family which had split into Maronite and Sunni wings. Lamartine described him as 'A Druze with Druze, a Christian with Christians and a Moslem with Moslems'. He was ready to do anything to establish his authority. It was Bashir who broke the feudal power of the Druze, albeit temporarily, and strengthened the power of the Maronites.

In 1843 Druze and Maronite domination of the mountains in Lebanon took the form of a twofold *'caimacamat'* system. Mount Lebanon was divided into two provinces, with the Maronites in the north and the Druze in the south. They were still under Ottoman authority but Russia and the Western Powers were already claiming the right to oversight of the region, and later, as we shall see, were to encourage the spread of confessionalism.

The Druze community were very involved in the struggle to end the mandate. Their numerical weakness was made up for by a fair degree of unity plus the fact that they were concentrated in one area and last but not least their very great fighting ability. There was a long established split between two clans, the Yazbakis, led by the Arslane family, and the Jumblatts, who gradually gained control of the community. From 1943 until his assassination by Syrian agents in 1977 Kemal Jumblatt was the most prestigious representative of the Druze community and at the same time the symbol of the left in Lebanon. It has proved difficult for the Progressive Socialist Party, founded by Jumblatt in 1949, to spread beyond its Druze origins, although some of its cadres are members of other religious communities. In passing it should be noted that there are also Druze communities in Syria and Israel.

The Maronites

The name of the largest Christian community in Lebanon comes from two monks. One of them, Marun, lived in the fifth Century. He was a pious and solitary figure and is held to be a saint by his followers. The other was Jean Maron, who lived in the seventh Century and was the real founder of the Maronite Church. Amongst his followers he encouraged monotheism which at that time was heretical. During this period the Maronites moved from Syria to Mount Lebanon to escape persecution at the hands of Orthodox Byzantine Christians. It was not until the time of the Crusades in the twelfth century that the Maronite church returned to the bosom of the Roman church. Even when it did so it retained its own liturgy.

Thus the fact that a Lebanese entity emerged was largely due to Maronite as well as Druze influence. In the period after 1920 they acquired a predominant influence in Lebanon under the mandate, thanks to the help of France and other Western countries.

A number of features are characteristic of the Maronites. Firstly they have a strong sense of community which they justify ideologically, as well as in their claims to 'Phoenician' origins. This is underlined by the fact that their numbers are heavily concentrated in certain areas, particularly in Mount Lebanon, as well as by their private Christian education system.

Secondly, they tend to look abroad for protection against the 'Muslim menace'. France is particularly well thought of in this context.

Thirdly, the Church, religious hierarchies and monastic orders play an important role in Maronite culture, and are subject to considerable manipulation by the big landowners.

Fourthly, there is a number of great families, whose power is based on the ownership of great estates, wealth, patronage and the 'historic heritage' to which they lay claim. These families exert a hold over economic, political and social life. The Frangieh family in Zghorta and the Eddes in the Bekaa Valley are two such families. They both have political parties which really exist to further family ambitions.

But the most distinctive feature of the Maronites lies in the existence of a community based party of a 'new type': the Phalange Party. It was founded on 21 November 1936 by a chemist, Pierre Gemayel, after he had been to Rome and visited the Olympic Games in Berlin. The 'Kataebs' were greatly influenced by fascist ideology and organisational methods. They reaffirmed their rejection of Arabism, their commitment to Lebanon's 'Phoenician' heritage, their support for private enterprise and their hostility to communism. At the beginning of the 1970s the Party had 70,000 members. It was the first party to set about organising its members militarily. 80% of them are Maronites, of petty bourgeois origins: white collar workers, craftspeople and shopkeepers. It is the most militant faction among the Maronites, demagogic in tone, and the sworn enemy of the great families. It has a limited but significant impact on traditional political life: in the 1972 elections it won 7 of the 99 seats. Since the start of the civil war and the polarisation which has taken place it has become the backbone of the right wing forces in the country. One of its members became president in 1982.

The Sunnis

The majority of the Muslims in the world are Sunnis. In Lebanon they form the third largest group in the population. As a result of an agreement in 1943 between prominent Maronite and Sunni families they made a decisive contribution to the move towards independence: the official Sunni position shifted from traditional pro-Syrian pan-Arabism to support for the idea of a Lebanese state.

The majority of Sunnis live in three towns: Beirut, Saida and Tripoli. The Sunni establishment, which chiefly consists of the industrial and commercial bourgeoisie, differs in two fundamental respects from the other religious oligarchies. They have no territorial power base much less any quasi-feudal or religious influence over their co-religionists. Furthermore there are a dozen important families – as opposed to two each for the Shiites and Druze – who are continually arguing over which of them should be the next prime minister. The Karamehs in Tripoli, the Salams in Beirut and the Solhs in Saida are amongst the most well known.

The ability to win the support of the urban masses is therefore vital if they are to retain their authority. To do so they adopt a more ideological approach than in rural areas, containing elements of Arab nationalism and Nasserism. The Sunni leaders keep the Muslim areas under tight control by using the help of *qabadays* who act rather like election agents, dispensing patronage and wielding powerful influence on behalf of their masters – whether upon the head of state, on the administration or on private business. However this system is slowly wearing away, partly because of the emergence of an intelligentsia, and the growing attraction of the Left and the P.L.O. The Sunni oligarchy's ascendancy was also due to their role as middlemen between Lebanon and the Arab political world in the 1940s and 1950s. Whatever vocation the Sunni families had in this field has been eroded as Lebanon and its different elite groups have remained unmoved while upheavals have taken place around them in the Middle East.

In contrast to the Shiites this weakening of the traditional leadership has not led to the appearance of a 'community' based party. The Sunnis are not a sufficiently homogenous group for that to happen. Initially they turned to the National Movement. After its failure in 1976 some people gave their support to religious leaders who had not previously been in the limelight. The most authorative religious leader in the country, Hassan Khalid, the Grand Mufti of Lebanon, acquired a new prominence in the 1970s.

The Shiites

The Shiites, dissenters from official Islam, have been in what is now Lebanon since the early centuries of the Hegira. There were a few Shiite Emirates in the 11th century but they were unimportant. The Shiites have often been persecuted, and only achieved recognition as a 'special group' in 1861. At the time of the French mandate the Shiites were the third largest group in the country and also the most deprived. This prompted mass emigration to Africa.

In 1943 they took part in the struggle to bring the French presence in Lebanon to an end. On independence they obtained the position of president of the parliament, and one fewer seat than the Sunnis. Their justifiable feeling of being under-represented has grown stronger since they became the largest religious group in the country.

The Shiites are in South Beirut, South Lebanon and the Bekaa Valley. They are the most deprived group in the country and are often likened to a separate, religiously-based social class. By way of illustration, 40% of industrial workers were Shiites when the Civil War broke out. But there are well-off Shiites: prominent quasi-feudal families in the South, forming an agrarian bourgeoisie engaged in the export business, with contacts among the people who emigrated to Africa. The Assads and the Hamads are the two clans which vie with each other to exert influence in the traditional manner.

The Shiites are by tradition rebellious and furnish the left and extreme left wing parties with many of their militant activists. The Communist Party of Lebanon is a notable case. At the end of the 1960s social and political frustrations led to a resurgence of life in the community; this was also sparked off by the fact that it was the Shiites who first and foremost bore the brunt of Israeli raids on South Lebanon. This resurgence was embodied in one man: Musa Sadr.

Sadr, a Lebanese from Iran, came to Lebanon in 1960 and adopted Lebanese nationality. He settled in Tyre where he succeeded to the place of the community's spiritual leader. He extended his range of activity from the religious to the social sphere, organising literacy classes, setting up schools and sports clubs, assisting poor families, and so on. After 1967 his efforts took on a political dimension. He set up the Shiite Supreme Council, becoming its president with the title of Imam in 1969. He denounced the country's failure to react to Israeli bombing raids. Whilst taking care not to isolate his movement from other religious groups, he put forward a programme aimed at mobilising all levels of the Shiite community. It advocated the right of Shiites to aspire to the highest office of state, assistance for the economic development of the South, protection of their religion from attack and so on. As Talal Jaber has stated in *Le Discours Shiite sur le Pouvoir* his aim 'seems to have been to thrust himself onto the Lebanese political stage in a way which was different from the traditional approach, yet retained some aspects of it. Traditionally there were two approaches: either that of the traditional political families who characterised Lebanese political life, or else the one adopted by the progressive parties whose restricted class-based appeal meant they were unable to gain entry to a political system which was based on religion'. What this meant was confrontation with both the traditional Shiite leaders and the left wing political parties.

The Imam set up the 'Disinherited People's Movement' which later became the Amal, which means hope, at meetings in Baalbec and Tyre just before the civil war broke out. Musa Sadr's death in Libya in 1978 did not mean the end of the organisation although it was temporarily weakened by his loss. The Amal became the first party since the Phalange to go beyond the confines of the great families without challenging the religious basis of the society.

In addition to these four main communities there are a number of others which have less political muscle. The Greek Orthodox community is numerically the fourth largest in the country. It is centred on Beirut and the Tripoli area, has close ties with the Arab world and shows little interest in Maronite appeals for Christian solidarity. The Orthodox and Catholic Armenians who sought refuge in Lebanon after being the victims of genocide try to stay neutral in the civil war. And there are also Greek Catholics, Protestants, Alawis, Nestorians and so on and so forth.

Estimated Communal Distribution of votes and deputies in Lebanon from 1960

| | CENSUS | | | | | | ESTIMATES | | | | | | | | 1960-1972 |
Religious Affiliation	1922		1932		1943 (1)		1956		1973 (3)		1975 (4)		1975 (5)		deputies
	votes	%	votes	%	votes	%	votes	%	votes	%	votes	%	votes	%	
Maronite	199 182	32.7	226.378	28.8	318 201	30.4	423 708	30	713 400	30.6	496 000	15.5	572 000	23	30
Greek orthodox	81 409	13.3	76 522	9.7	106 658	10.2	148 927	10.6	261 580	11.2	230 000	7.2	175 000	7	11
Greek-catholic	41 426	7.0	46 000	5.9	61 956	5.9	87 788	6.2	142 680	6.1	213 000	6.6	124 000	5	6
Others (mainly Armenians)	12 651	2.1	53 463	6.8	64 603	6.2	109 135	7.7	142 680	6.1	260 000	8.1	124 000	5	7
Total Christians	334 668	55.1	402 363	51.2	551 418	52.7	769 558	54.7	1 260 340	54	1 199 000	37.4	995 000	40	54
Sunni	124 786	20.5	175 925	22.4	222 594	21.3	285 698	20.3	475 600	20.4	690 000	21.5	646 000	26	20
Shiite	104 947	17.2	154 208	19.6	200 698	19.2	250 605	17.8	451 820	19.4	970 000	30.2	671 000	27	19
Druze	43 633	7.2	53 047	6.8	71 711	6.9	88 131	6.3	142 680	6.2	348 000	10.9	174 000	7	6
Total Muslims	273 366	44.9	383 180	48.8	495 003	47.3	624 434	44.3	1 070 100	46	2 008 000	62.6	1 491 000	60	45
TOTAL	608 034	100	785 543	100	1 046 421	100	1 393 992	100	2 330 440	100	3 207 000	100	2 486 000	100	99

Divisions Along Religious Lines

One of the most essential aspects of Mount Lebanon is its geography. Within these inaccessible mountains natural shelter can be found for persecuted minorities, whether Maronite, Druze, Shiite or anyone else. True, it is not unique in this respect. For example, the position is similar in the mountains of Kurdistan. The 'millet' system which was set up under Ottoman rule at the beginning of the sixteenth century provided for the recognition of non-Muslim cities existing alongside the ones under Muslim administration. Their religious leaders enjoyed many privileges and exercised control over the lives of their flock. Traces of this long tradition of coexistence between communities living alongside each other remain in people's outlook. They emphasise the political role of the religious hierarchies.

Religious-based divisions spread particularly rapidly in the nineteenth century as a result of the direct intervention by the colonial powers. The Druze, nominally Muslims, had been the first to acquire special status under the twin *caimacamat* arrangement. This movement was spurred on by the events of 1860. At first it was a peasants' revolt against their feudal masters, led by a blacksmith named Tanios Shahine. It began in the Christian area and spread to the Druze region where the majority of peasants were Maronites. Faced with the danger that the conflict would spread, the Druze feudal landlords called on their co-religionists to support them. The Maronite clergy responded on similar lines. What began as a peasants revolt became a religious war. The massacre of thousands of Christians was an adequate excuse for Napolean III to send in an expeditionary force which arrived well after the fighting had ended and had to make do with mopping up what was left of the insurrectionary peasants.

In the lights of these events the Mount Lebanon issue became a European matter. In June 1861 an agreement was reached which provided for the establishment of 'Lesser Lebanon', from which 4,500 square kilometres of the present country were excluded. Subject to modification in 1864, it was still the same in 1914. Mount

Lebanon was to be an autonomous region directly answerable to the Ottoman authorities who in turn undertook to always appoint Christian governments. An administrative council was set up, comprising representatives of the six main religious groups: Maronites, Druze, Sunni Muslims, Shiites, Greek Orthodox and Greek Catholics. The region was divided up into seven '*mudiriyas*': four of them Maronite, one Druze, one Greek Orthodox and one Greek Catholic. This gave an overwhelming influence in the area to the Christians and Maronites. The imposition of this partition strengthened the religiously based nature of political and social life. For the first time Muslims, in this case the Shiites, were considered to be like the Druze – outsiders. The accentuation of the differences between communities was further underlined when the Western powers each took it upon themselves to act as protector to the various communities: Britain took the Druze under its wing, France the Maronites, and Russia the Greek Orthodox.

Things changed in 1920: the French mandate over the region was established and Greater Lebanon – which corresponds to the present-day country – was carved out at the expense of Syria. Divisions along religious lines were strengthened in three ways. Christians were only just in the majority in the new country, and fear of being swamped by the 'enemy' drew them closer together. At the beginning of 1926 the Shiites acquired full status as a separate community, which removed them from their previous dependence on the Sunnis. And, finally, Article 95 of the 1926 constitution stated that – as a temporary measure – each community would have equal representation in public sector employment and ministerial posts. Sixty years later this 'temporary' arrangement is still in operation. As laid down by the mandate each community is autonomous in legal and judicial areas relating to personal matters such as marriage, divorce, and inheritance. To this day there is no such thing as marriage by civil ceremony. Thus divisions between the community do not just persist, they are getting deeper. They have not stopped the shared struggle for independence but they have limited its range and impact.

A Historic Compromise

The independence of Lebanon was proclaimed on 22 November 1943. The new country's territory included Mount Lebanon, the coastal plain, Beirut, the Bekaa Valley and the area around Tripoli. In the first part of the book we looked at the circumstances in which France was forced to abandon its Middle Eastern possessions as the result of wide-ranging popular struggle, but there was another aspect as well: a 'national pact', which, though it never existed in written form, represented a compromise between the main Christian and Muslim families whose interests are predominant in Lebanon. The first part of the agreement provided for the Christians to give up French protection in exchange for the Muslims giving up claims to Arab unity, and unity with Syria as the first step towards it. A Lebanese observer writing at the time showed some foresight in pointing out that 'a country is not made up of two denials'. Another element involved in the birth of the new state was to be the maintenance of divisions on religious lines. All state positions and jobs in the public sector were to be allocated on religious lines. So, in the parliament, six out of every eleven seats go to Christians and five to Muslims. These are in turn subdivided amongst each religious sub-group. The pact provides for the President of the Republic and the Army Chief of Staff to be Maronites, the Prime Minister to be a Sunni, and for a Shiite to be President of Parliament. The posts of Parliamentary Vice-President of Parliament and, more importantly, Minister of Foreign Affairs go to members of the Greek Orthodox community. Other governmental and administrative jobs are also subject to the same criteria, though not quite so rigidly.

The Presidential nature of the regime means that the Maronites have what amounts to hegemony over the country. The President is elected by the members of parliament for a period of six years and is not answerable to them. He enjoys real power, as the country's recent history has shown. The highly complex electoral system gives rise to all sorts of abuse, and to gerrymandering, by influential families and clans. As A. Bourgi and P. Weiss point out in their book *Les Complots Libanais* what has happened over the decades since the country achieved independence is the evolution of a kind of 'genealogical parliament': 'Emile Edde was succeeded by his two sons, Raymond and Pierre, Ahmed Assad's son Kamel took over his father's "political heritage", and in the future Bashir and Amin Gemayel will carry on from their father Pierre, as will Suleiman Frangieh's son Tony, and Camille Chamoun's sons Dany and Dory'. Thirty years after independence part of the population rose up against the rigidity of this system based on tradition and religion.

However it did have the strength of its weaknesses: during the 1950s and 60s these customs and conventions meant that there was relative political freedom, which was unheard of in the Arab countries. Beirut became a centre of argument not just for Lebanon but for opponents of all the regimes in the area.

In 1943 the newly created state of Lebanon was still largely traditional. Although agriculture only represented a small part of G.D.P. – less than 20% – over half the workforce were engaged in it. It was a rural society, based on the family in terms of property and the organisation of work, and on patronage. This patronage took the form of a kind of a barter: a leading figure – or member of parliament – was able to strengthen his position in the community in exchange for the services he rendered in fields such as employment, housing, or the law. Bourgeois businessmen were able to enhance their position as a result of the Second World War. The creation of the state of Israel and the end of Haifa as a regional competitor for the port of Beirut meant that Lebanon acquired a virtual monopoly position as a go-between for European capitalism and the Arab world. This has left its mark on the Lebanese bourgeoisie and, through them, on the country.

A Fool's Paradise

The history of Lebanon since the war has been a chronicle of growing contradictions between the original characteristics which we have just outlined and developments on a national and regional level which have shaken them.

The fragile social and religious equilibrium which the Maronite and Sunni oligarchies had managed to set up was not strong enough to withstand the rapid changes which took place in the country. The last official census which serves as the basis for official business dates back as far as 1932! Lebanon has been very sensitive to what has happened in the surrounding region and this has proved fatal during a thirty year period when the Arab world has been continually subject to unrest and upheaval.

Lebanon transformed itself in the thirty years preceding the 1975 explosion. The oil boom boosted its role as the stopping off point in the region between the Arab economies and Western Europe and the United States. Lebanon's free market liberalism attracted capital from the Gulf States or from investors getting out of the socialist grip in Egypt, Syria and Iraq. In 1970 the service sector – banking, finance, commerce and tourism – accounted for 70% of G.N.P., one of the highest figures in the world. Beirut was also the place where many service industries set up in business, where they became hegemonic, particularly in the banking sector. This growth brought with it real prosperity, but it was unequally distributed. The state took no part in this, which meant that nothing was done to reduce flagrant social inequalities. This disparity in wealth followed religious lines, but only to a certain extent; this served to make it all the more difficult to distinguish just where the religious and the political overlapped.

Lebanon's dependence on the capitalist countries and the Arab world can be seen in the foreign trade figures: at the beginning of the 1970s 70% of imports came from the West while 60% of exports went to the Middle East. The growing trade deficit was more than made up for by a strong balance of payments surplus due to Lebanon's position as a financial centre, income from tourism, and capital sent home by people working abroad.

Even though the bulk of capital was not invested in production, industry did undergo remarkable expansion. The industrial workforce rose from 35,000 in 1953 to 135,000 in 1975, almost 20% of the working population. The traditional and modern sectors continued to co-exist, but at the expense of the former. Capitalism penetrated into the rural areas and changed traditional social relations. There was a growing exodus to the towns, and notably to Beirut, where 60% of all the country's industry was now centred. In 1970 60% of the population lived in towns. Today that figure has been exceeded, with the influx of refugees from South Lebanon, firstly people fleeing Israeli raids and then the Israeli army. The capital is surrounded by a poverty belt in which the opposition, and Amal in particular, have found lasting mass support.

Industrial development has led to a certain degree of religious integration. But it has come up against the Lebanese system: fundamental social relations such as marriage and divorce are part of a strong religious framework. Getting a job in the public sector and even in the private sector – where employers tend to favour people of their own religion – perpetuates the sharp divisions which stem from educational inequality.

Despite these constraints social movements have had considerable impact. At the beginning of the 1960s a number of strikes occurred, notably in the state-controlled tobacco business, electricity and in private companies. The peasants were not excluded either: their actions set off a chain of events that built up into the civil war: a strike in a food factory in Ghandour in 1972, a general strike in August 1973, as well as the tobacco workers' struggle and the creation of the Federation of Agricultural Workers in the same year and so on. These political movements had some impact on the elections of 1972, which were the last to take place. The Left made considerable gains despite the electoral system. A young Nasserite candidate was elected in Beirut, beating a traditional figure; a Baathist won in Tripoli; in the South a Communist Party of Lebanon candidate obtained 10,324 votes against 14,658 for Kamel Assad – the most powerful clan chief in the region.

So despite the obstacles things began to come to the boil in Lebanon. Demographic changes meant that the inequality between the different groups was no longer tolerable. But it was because of other events elsewhere in the region, and the appearance of the Palestinian resistance, that the situation in Lebanon erupted.

The Palestinian Dimension

The upheavals of 1975-76 were not bolts out of the blue.
Once before, in 1958, civil war had already shown the
weakness of the Lebanese state. In order to keep the ship
of state afloat Chamoun had had to call in American
marines. On that occasion the outcome was six months of
unrest, 2,000 dead and the election as president of the
Army Chief of Staff, Fuad Chebab. In the recent
upheavals the combination of internal and external
elements proved, tragically, to be even more explosive.

The 1967 war and its aftermath brought to an end the
uneasy peace that had followed the restoration of order in
1958. Although Lebanon was the only one of Israel's
neighbours to escape unscathed, it could not ignore the
resurgence of Palestinian resistance that Israeli aggression
provoked. For the Palestinians Lebanon had been a very
important refuge from 1948 onwards. Apart from a
privileged few they had been dumped there in camps in
the southern part of the country where they lived in
poverty, subject to abuse and exploitation, as well as to
needling from the military authorities. All forms of
political and, of course, military activity were forbidden.
After the Six Day War Palestinian commandos galvanised
the Arab masses. Although based in Jordan they began to
establish themselves in Lebanon. Israel responded with
increasingly harsh reprisal raids. The first one took place
in June 1968. In December that year virtually all
Lebanon's commercial aircraft were destroyed. The Tel
Aviv government was not so much seeking to destroy the
fedayin – its targets were often both Lebanese and civilian
– as to force the Lebanese government to take action
against them. This tactic, which worked in Jordan, failed
in Lebanon. It simply precipitated Lebanon's decomposition.

The first real crisis between the resistance and the state
occurred in October 1968. With the backing of a
broadly-based Lebanese mass movement expressing both
social grievances and national aspirations, the fedayin
were able to achieve formal recognition of their presence
in the country under the terms of the Cairo Accords of

November 1969. This arrangement was approved by almost all the political forces in the country, including the kataebs, but it was from this moment onwards that the right wing parties began to set up armed militias. After the P.L.O. was destroyed in Jordan in 1970-71 Lebanon became the Palestinians last base. The resistance became firmly established while the failure of both the military and the government to face up to increasingly frequent Israeli raids gave rise to vigorous argument amongst the Lebanese themselves. On the night of 9-10 August 1973, elite Israeli commandos landed in Beirut, assassinated three important P.L.O. and Fatah leaders and got away again without any difficulty. Accusations of incompetence or, worse still, complicity were levelled against the Lebanese army. The prime minister, Saeb Salam, resigned. A quarter of a million Lebanese and Palestinians attended the funerals on 12 April.

This was more than President Frangie would put up with: in May 1973 he launched an attack on the P.L.O. It was not successful but it served to widen divisions within the country. It was not just the presence of the P.L.O. that was at stake: so was the very confessionalism on which the country was based. Already shaken by local tensions, the alliance between the Left and the P.L.O. now threatened to finish it once and for all. It was in the light of this danger and in order 'to defend Christianity' that the Phalangists and their allies now mobilised. Everything was ready for a civil war.

Civil War

The bloodiest ever conflict in the country known as the 'Switzerland of the Middle East' arose from the combination of a number of factors: economic and social crisis, increasing Palestinian radicalism, and the steadfast determination of the Maronite bourgeoisie to hold on to their privileges. Furthermore these potentially explosive elements should be seen in the light of a new regional context: by the beginning of 1975 the idea of an International Middle East Peace Conference was just a memory. Kissinger's painstaking 'step-by-step' strategy had led to a disengagement agreement which preceded the formal ending of hostilities between Israel and Egypt on 1 September 1975. Seen from this angle the P.L.O. presence in Lebanon and its alliance with the Lebanese Left were the last obstacle in the way of a 'Pax Americana'. Any move to get rid of it met with Washington's approval.

The 'official' date when the civil war began was 13 April 1975, when a bus returning Palestinians and Lebanese to the Sabra Camp passed through the Phalangist-controlled Ail el Remmaneh district. In a sudden hail of gunfire 27 passengers were killed. Reprisals and counter-reprisals followed and fighting spread through the country. It marked a new chapter in Lebanese history.

Two far from homogenous blocks confronted each other during the civil war: the Lebanese Front and the Lebanese National Movement. Between the two were a wide range of groups and individuals whose position was not clearly defined and whom we shall call 'floaters'.

The Lebanese Front (L.F.), officially formed nine months after the start of hostilities, was made up of four parts all of whom were Christian, not to say Maronite: the clan led by President Suleiman Frangieh plus that of ex-President Camille Chamoun who had 3,500 militia known as the Tigers; in addition there was Father Kassis, the leader of the Conference of Monastic Orders, and finally the Phalange Party led by Pierre Gemayel whose 15,000 men were the mainstay of the right wing coalition. The Lebanese National Movement (L.N.M.) was made up of about fifteen parties going from the centre-left to the ultra-left. It included many different religious denominations, and had some influence in the Christian, particularly Greek Orthodox communities. Its unchallenged leader and the key figure in the coalition was Kemal Jumblatt. His party, the Progressive Socialist Party (P.S.P.), and its 3,000-strong militia, was the main fighting force of the L.N.M. The Communist Party was another member of the coalition and along with the Syrian National Social Party was notable for being non-denominational. Its political and ideological influence can be seen in many of the coalition's decisions. In addition to these groups there were the Lebanese Communist Action Organisation

(L.C.A.O.), the pro-Syrian Baathists, the Morabituns, a Sunni-based Nasserite Movement, and several other groups. The L.N.M. opposed not only the Lebanese Right, but also the Sunni and Shiite establishments who saw the L.N.M. as vying with them for the support of the Muslim communities. Despite contradictory declarations the aims of the two sides can be summed up as follows: getting rid of the Palestinians, and setting up a federal or, if necessary, Maronite state on the one hand: and alliance with the Palestinian resistance and secularisation of the country on the other.

Between these two blocks lay what we shall call the 'floaters', prominent among whom were the traditional leaders of the Muslim community. They had little time for the socio-economic aspirations of the masses and claimed to stand by the provisions of the national pact while demanding minor changes in, for example, the balance of power between the president and the prime minister, and advocating a fairer distribution of jobs in the civil service. Their concern about the influence of the L.N.M. led them to adopt more radical slogans, at least at the start of the war, in an effort to maintain their influence over the Muslim masses. There were also floaters from the other side – Raymond Edde for example, who sought to distance himself from the policies of the L.F. Party leaders representing other Christian groups, such as the Armenians and the Greek Orthodox Church, were in a similar 'floating' position. A special place must be set aside for the 'Disinherited Movement' who fought with the L.N.M. until the break with Syria. It would not be possible in this context to cover each stage of the civil war. All we can do is point out some aspects of it. The Palestinians, or more precisely the P.L.O. leadership, made sure that they did not fall into a trap. The 'rejectionists' were alone in allying themselves with the L.N.M. from the outset. The P.L.O. did not get involved in the fighting until January 1976 when the L.F. attacked the Palestinian camps in Beirut. It had no alternative. The support of the Palestinian resistance tilted the balance of power in favour of the L.N.M. For a time victory seemed within their grasp. At this juncture the Damascus government

intervened, politically at first and then miltarily. At the
time the Syrian leaders were negotiating with Kissinger.
They hoped to reach a compromise with the United States
and to retrieve the Golan Heights. They were also
concerned at the prospect of a 'revolutionary' regime in
Lebanon, which they viewed as a 'security zone' for Syria.
And there were some people in Damascus who still argued
that the 1920 'imperialist' partition which had cut Lebanon
off from the 'mother country' could be reversed. The
myth of 'Greater Syria' was particularly alive and well at
this period.

On 1 June 1976 Syrian troops entered Lebanon in
strength. They acted in conjunction with the Phalangists to
crush the L.N.M. and the P.L.O. The Tal el Zaater camp
fell on 12 August 1976. In mid-October Saudi Arabia held
an Arab mini-summit. In addition to the Saudi hosts,
representatives from Kuwait, the P.L.O., Egypt, Syria and
the new president of Lebanon, Elias Sarkis, took part. It
resulted in a ceasefire: the fifty-sixth in less than eighteen
months. This saved the L.N.M. and the P.L.O. but
legitimised the Syrian presence in the country. With the
symbolic addition of contingents from other Arab
countries the Syrian troops were renamed the Arab
Dissuasion Force (A.D.F.), and were placed under the
formal command of the Lebanese president. For a time
the L.F. rejected an agreement which seemed to deprive it
of victory, but it very soon had to accept it. The A.D.F.,
whose ostensible function was to help bring about a return
to law and order, took up positions throughout the
country, except in the South because of strong Israeli
objections. Officially speaking the civil war was at an end.

The country was like a battlefield: 30,000 dead, twice
that number wounded. 600,000 people had fled their
homes, their districts or their villages. The country's
economic, particularly industrial, potential had been hard
hit. The most optimistic estimates calculated it would take
five years to get back to 1974 levels – providing that
fighting stopped.

In comparison to 1958 the country was not just worse
off: at the end of the war it was literally in tatters.
President Frangieh's willingness to use the army against

the L.N.M. and the P.L.O. had so destroyed its unity that it
was now split into three fragments. One was still neutral;
one, under the leadership of Antoine Barakat, had joined
the Phalangists; and the third part, now calling itself the
Lebanese Arab Army, had joined the L.N.M. And this is
not to mention the soldiers who had quite simply gone
home. For the new president, Sarkis, the number one task
on the agenda for national reconstruction was to
reconstitute the army.

Another consequence of the civil war which now
threatened Lebanon was the deeping of denominational
divisions. The L.F. had made great use of this tactic to
draw the Maronites together, with horrific consequences:
massacres started to occur. On 6 December 1975 the
Phalangists killed 200 people in Beirut for the 'crime' of
possessing an identity card stating that they were Muslims.
At the beginning of 1976 the Quarantaine Camp was
attacked and hundreds of civilians, including many
Palestinians, murdered. In a country in which religious
affiliation was so deeply rooted these massacres inevitably
prompted reprisals, despite the efforts of the L.N.M.
leadership to stop them. Terror and war gave added
impetus to internal migration as people moved to areas
which were steadily becoming religiously homogenous. At
this point we should note that in Beirut, the capital, the
exclusively Christian Eastern part of the city came under
Phalangist control and that all the other religious groups
coexisted in the Western part.

Three factors accentuated this deterioration which may
well bring about the end of Lebanon. Firstly the defeat of
the L.N.M., an opponent of divisions on religious lines, In
its 28 June 1977 programme it came out against
'confessional partitions' and in favour of 'a political
formula for a national equilibrium that will enable all
categories and forces within Lebanon to participate
democratically in the institutions of power'. But for the
time being the L.N.M. was no longer in the driving seat.
The victorious L.F. now aimed higher still. Rejecting the
1943 status quo, they proposed that the country should be
split up into Christian and Muslim dominated cantons,
and that the federal state institutions should also be

divided up on regional lines. Encouraged by the Arab
countries, the traditional Muslim leaders meanwhile made
use of the situation to re-establish their positions. For them
it was a case of some good coming from misfortune.

The third consequence of the civil war was in the South.
The Israelis had forbidden any A.D.F. presence but had
set up their own security zone as early as the summer of
1976. Israeli-trained and equipped Christian militia led by
Major Saad Haddad patrolled the frontier zone. When the
Likud gained power the Israeli army intervened more and
more frequently. Following the spring 1978 invasion, the
area came to symbolise the running sore of the Lebanese
crisis. The Israeli government had no scruples about
stirring up the conflict and blocking any political peace
move in Beirut. It was already clear at this stage that there
were two alternatives which would be the object of future
Israeli policy: either a strong Phalangist-controlled state
and no P.L.O., or else Israel could gamble on continuing
factionalism while still backing the Phalangists.

The Phoney Civil War

The 'no war, no peace' situation went on until the Israeli
invasion in 1982. Although no major changes in either the
security or the authority of the state took place during the
Sarkis presidency (1976 to 1982), a number of significant
regional and local developments did occur. Syria had
incurred considerable hostility in the Arab world following
its invasion of Lebanon, and now sought to repair some of
that damage and to enhance her pan-Arab prestige. The
special relationship between Israel and the L.F. went very
much against the grain. But more importantly it was the
end of the Kissinger era. Sadat's trip to Jerusalem, and the
Camp David Agreements, triggered an about-turn in
Baathist policy. Now that Washington had turned to Cairo
as its partner in the next peace offensive, Damascus was in
danger of finding itself completely isolated. So it switched
allies. Friction with the L.F. turned into armed confrontation from the beginning of 1978. There was a real
rapprochement with the L.N.M. However in what was
referred to at the time, in 1982, as a 'startlingly self-critical'

statement George Hawi, the General Secretary of the Lebanese Communist Party said that 'Syria has always tried to keep a number of cards in its hands in this conflict, and even to consider Lebanon as a card to be used in Syria's interests in the wider regional context'. He goes on to say that Syria could never favour 'a Lebanese national movement that was truly autonomous, and independent in its decisions, positions and action'.

Another aspect of the development of the Lebanese question was change within the L.F. After the break with Syria it split. Frangieh, an ally of Damascus, left, and wasted no time in joining the other side. Meanwhile the L.F. became more 'radical'. 'Friendship' with Tel Aviv became the cornerstone of its policy. Any form of compromise that did not include expelling the Palestinians was rejected. The symbol of this new line was an ambitious, unscrupulous young leader named Bashir Gemayel. He was appointed as Chief of the Lebanese Armed Forces in August 1976 and rapidly set about unifying all its military units. He was not frightened of using violence, even against his allies, as in, for example, the liquidation of the Chamoun militia during the summer of 1980. He turned the Christian enclave into a veritable mini-state in which the bayonet was boss. In 1981, strengthened by these 'achievements', and with Israeli support, he began a campaign aimed at becoming head of state.

The anarchic situation enabled the P.L.O. to carve out an enclave for itself which George Hawi describes as 'a mini-state on Lebanese soil, operating outside the law of the land, taking upon itself the exercise of power in many parts of the country, over Lebanese citizens as well as Palestinians and even over the L.N.M. itself'. In this lay the origins of the break between the Palestinian resistance on one side with the bulk of the Palestinians and the Lebanese on the other. This gulf steadily widened as the population of South Lebanon suffered badly from Israeli reprisals and fighting between different Palestinian factions.

The troubles of the L.N.M., already weakened by the assassination of its leader Kemal Jumblatt in March 1977, now got worse. The list of setbacks was a long one: defeat

in 1976, extortion at the hands of both Palestinian and
L.N.M. forces, the spread of religious divisions, and so on.
The religious divide seemed to have deepened to such an
extent that even the L.N.M. gave in to it. According to
Hawi 'it meant that the legitimate demands of the
Muslims for religious equality seemed initially to be the
only form of opposition to the fascist proposals. So much
for the democratic secular struggle ... The National
Movement came to be seen as tied to the Muslim religious
movement, as though it were now linked to one of the two
sides in the traditional Lebanese bipolarisation'.

When they invaded Lebanon on 6 June 1982 the Israeli
leaders certainly expected to pluck the country like a ripe
fruit. Their disappointment was to be all the more bitter
because of their wildly optimistic expectations.

Lost Opportunities

Israel's military stroll through South Lebanon began well
enough. In five days the Israeli army was at the gates of
Beirut. Syria accepted American guarantees about Israel
not going beyond a fictional 40 kilometre limit, and did
not seek to confront the Israeli forces. Its army was
destroyed nevertheless and a ceasefire signed on 11 June.
The P.L.O., thinking that what was happening was a
repeat of 1978, withdrew its forces from the South. Some
factions within the L.N.M. thought resistance was
pointless. Druze Israelis approached their Lebanese
co-religionists and negotiated a way into the Shouf
mountain stronghold of the Jumblatts, which fell without a
shot being fired.

However the P.L.O. leaders and the L.N.M. groups
soon realised the scale of Israeli ambitions. They resolved
to hold Beirut come what may. For nearly three months
the Lebanese and Palestinian fighters under Yasser
Arafat's leadership held out against the strongest military
force in the Middle East. Saturation bombing and
anti-personnel weapons were unable to defeat them.
When the P.L.O. men left the capital at the end of August
they did so having won a political victory, while Israel had
suffered its first military setback in its campaign in

Lebanon. It was not the last one. Bashir Gemayel, whose election to the presidency had taken place under Israeli military protection, never took up his office. He was assassinated on 14 September. At first his death seemed to mark the beginning of the end of the Lebanese civil war. People of all religious beliefs and political affiliations longed for peace, with no winners and no losers. There was a kind of national consensus over the election of Amin Gemayel as president. The different forces called for a united, sovereign Lebanon and the withdrawal of all foreign troops. It seemed to be the beginning of an *'entente nationale'*.

However this was not how the Israelis and the Phalangists saw it. The state and army were reconstructed in a way that benefitted only one section of the community: all the leading positions went to Phalangists. More and more attacks on Muslim Palestinian and progressive activists occurred. Provocative Phalangist action in the Shouf Mountains became increasingly frequent as they tried to gain a foothold there. But there was another element in the post 1982 period – the change in the situation in occupied South Lebanon. The mainly Shiite population had initially responded to the Israeli invasion by keeping relatively quiet. However, after enduring a year of occupation, on 6 June 1983, the whole population came together to demonstrate their rejection of prolonged foreign occupation.

In this tense atmosphere, on 17 May 1983 Amin Gemayel signed an agreement with Israel, with American backing; this was a triple provocation. Firstly, it was a rebuff to the international forum which had demanded unconditional Israeli withdrawal from Lebanon. Secondly, the opposition parties were neither consulted about it nor associated with it. And lastly it was a provocation to Syria, whose interests the agreement threatened. For President Gemayel signing the Lebanon-Israel agreement was to boomerang: the opposition set up the National Salvation Front which was the broadest alliance seen in Lebanon for twenty years. It brought together Walid Jumblatt's P.S.P., the Communist Party, the head of the Sunnis in Tripoli Rashid Karameh, and the northern Maronite leader

Suleiman Frangieh. Other groups backed the Front
without becoming members, most notably Nabih Berri's
Amal militia. Syria also came down on their side,
providing political and military backing for the opposition
to Amin Gemayel.

In the space of a few months the situation was completely
reversed. The Druze and the P.S.P. won the 'War in the
Mountains' in the autumn of 1983, while the Amal militia
seized West Beirut in February 1984. The government
resigned, the army fell apart. The contingents that made
up the multinational force, led by U.S. marines, had to
leave Beirut. The Lebanon-Israel agreement, which had
never been ratified by the Lebanese parliament was
rescinded on 7 March. On 26 April Rashid Karameh was
asked to lead a government of national unity in which
Walid Jumblatt and Nabih Berri were to serve. Amin
Gemayel abandoned his alliance with Israel and turned to
the Syrians, who, buoyed up by their success, now saw
their role as 'protectors' of the newly established balance of
power.

What most concerned the political forces in Lebanon
was to liberate the South. A new round of negotiations
with Israel began in the small town of Nagora but no
agreement was reached. The Lebanese position was much
strengthened by resistance successes against the Israeli
army, and by Israeli public opinion which was clamouring
for the soldiers to be brought home. The armed struggle,
which the communists and the left had begun, widened in
the summer of 1983 when the Amal joined in. It forced
the Israeli leaders to undertake a unilateral withdrawal,
which was accompanied by bloody repression. Israel
announced that the evacuation was over on 6 June 1985,
but in reality it still controls a six to ten kilometre-deep
buffer zone all along the frontier and has several hundred
military 'advisers' operating with the South Lebanese
Army (S.L.A.).

The semi-liberation of the country has not, however,
solved Lebanon's internal problems. The government of
national unity has not been able to draw up the necessary
reforms. There is a total impasse, despite the weakness of
the (Phalangist) Lebanese Forces. Religious massacres and

the exodus of tens of thousands of people from the
country have accentuated the process of division into
denominational zones. Syria, playing one faction off
against another and making sure that no one group gains
the upper hand, appears to be the only power able to
maintain any semblance of unity in the country.
Anti-Palestinian chauvinism – with the Amal and the army
joining together to lay siege to the camps in Beirut –
though shared by all sectors of public opinion, will not be
enough to bring about a return of national unity.
Although, some six years after the Israeli army's
invasion of Lebanon, it is clear that the Israeli and
Phalangist strategy has failed, the very least one can say is
that a united, democratic and secular Lebanon is still a far
off dream.

Chapter 5

Strategic Confrontation

Having looked at the Arab-Israeli conflict from the Israeli, Palestinian and Lebanese points of view, it is now appropriate to look at its regional and international dimensions. Here, as elsewhere, and perhaps even more so here, because of geopolitical considerations, there is continued interaction between the local and global levels.

As Eric Rouleau pointed out in a recent article in *Le Monde Diplomatique* ' ... all civil wars attract foreign intervention just as lightning conductors attract lightning'. After referring to the civil war which ravaged the USSR at the end of the First World War, the Spanish and Greek Wars which preceded and followed the Second World War, as well as those in the Congo, Vietnam and Nigeria, he goes on to say: 'The destabilising effects of local conflicts stimulate greed and open the door to outside interference. The extent of interference is determined by the range of interests in question. When necessary these interests become 'vital'. In the past the imperial powers justified their military adventures on the noble grounds of needing to protect the Christians within the Ottoman Empire from the threat of massacre. In the more refined context of the twentieth century the pretexts have become less gross, or at least a little more believable for our contemporaries. Among such pretexts are stopping a rival's 'hegemonic aims', or 'subversive activity', or preventing them from taking part in civil wars – whether real or imaginary – the existence of which can be either denied or played down'.

This fifth and final part of the book is concerned with

intervention at both global and regional levels: the USA and the USSR on one hand, Egypt, Jordan, Saudi Arabia, Iraq and Syria on the other. It is much easier to explain the strategy they have adopted in the past, as we have done in detail in previous chapters, than it is to explain their position today. This is an even more difficult task given the upheavals taking place in the Middle East as this book goes to press. Developments in the situation in Lebanon, and the Reagan plan's lack of progress, represent a serious setback for the United States. In the light of events we should avoid hasty judgements. Similarly it would be imprudent to underestimate the changes taking place in the Egyptian and Syrian regimes, although they may well prove to be reversible. To sum up, without the benefit of foresight we should tread cautiously.

Oil and Other Things

The Middle East has a number of exceptional features which have for centuries made it a highly desirable region. It is still the case today, perhaps even more than before.

Credit where credit is due: oil, the area's main resource, is also what is at stake in the rivalry between the imperialist powers. Certainly its importance has slightly declined in recent years, as the graph on p. 000 illustrates. The arrival on the scene of new, non-Arab producers, and above all the increasing use of alternative sources of energy – chiefly nuclear energy – has meant that OPEC has had to face up to competition. Nevertheless it retains a strong position. In 1983 according to the Professional Oil Committee the Middle East accounted for 21.99% of world oil output (30.57% excluding the socialist countries), 55.3% of world oil reserves (63.2% excluding the socialist countries), and 24.22% of world gas reserves (44.21% excluding the socialist countries). 59% of oil supplied to O.E.C.D. countries came from the Arab world.

The size of the market that these countries represent has grown at the same pace as the expansion of their financial resources. Like all barely-developed regions, the Arab world, with its 100,000,000 people (excluding those in North Africa) has enormous needs in terms of its

Production of Crude Oil from 1970 to 1982
(in millions of tonnes)

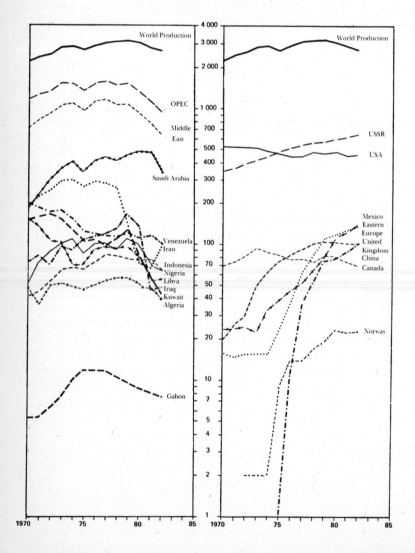

infrastructure, heavy industry, light industry and consumer goods. With the rise in oil prices after the 1973 war,
their purchasing power rose substantially. The pro-
Western outlook of most of the countries in the region
naturally led them to turn to the Western capitalist
countries for help. The famous petro-dollar surplus (in
1980, according to OPEC, this amounted to 120 billion
dollars, two thirds of which came from the Arab world) is
invested in the American and Western European
economies. Two more figures give an idea of the enormity
of the sums involved: in 1980 the total value of American
exports to the Arab world amounted to 11 billion dollars;
and the sum total of Arab capital investment in the United
States was over 130 billion dollars. Restricted production
and stagnant prices have now stemmed the flow of cash.

The Middle East's magnetic attraction for would-be
hegemonic ambitions is also due to its strategic importance. It is the meeting point of three separate cross
currents: Europe, Asia and Africa, the North and the
South and the East and the West. Ever since the Russian
revolution the West has seen it as the boundary of the
Soviet Union's southern flank. Despite the drop in
merchant shipping, and the fact that supertankers are
obliged to go via the Cape of Good Hope, the Middle East
and the Suez Canal is still the quickest route between the
Mediterranean and the Indian Ocean.

Oil, commercial markets, and strategic considerations:
control of the Middle East is a prerequisite for any
aspirations to world domination. The Ancients discovered
this. The nineteenth century colonial powers followed in
their footsteps. The United States policy is following the
same path.

The Killjoys

As the twentieth century wore on, the great powers' bitter
struggle for regional hegemony took on another aspect:
firm resistance to Arab independence movements.

Up until the First World War, as we have seen, Britain,
France, Tsarist Russia and Germany vied with each other
over the amount of goodies each would get from the

Ottoman Empire, and often manipulated the infant nationalist movements to serve their own interests. Between the
wars Britain consolidated its position at the expense of
France and Germany. The United States appeared on the
oil horizon. The Soviet Union, while not neglecting diplomacy, had abandoned the old Tsarist aims and given its
backing to the growing revolutionary movements. These
efforts bore fruit on its borders but not with the Arab
countries. Strong popular support for independence
movements in Syria, Egypt and Iraq in the 1920s and 1930s
certainly spoilt things for imperialism. Opposition to
Britain, as the main imperialist oppressor, and the pro-
German views held by some of the leaders, caused the
movement to go off course at the beginning of the Second
World War.

   The political scene was completely changed by the defeat
of the fascist powers. The birth of Israel provided the
Western powers with a reliable ally. They would guarantee
the survival and expansion of Israel come what may. But
this fanned the flames of Arab radical nationalism. Hostility
to Zionism strengthened anti-imperialism. The United
States was worried about the part played by the Soviet
Union in the defeat of Nazism and the popular prestige it
had in the region. Thus, in the post-war period it became
heavily involved in the area, taking over from traditional
British and French colonialism. After the Franco-British
Suez disaster, the United States held virtually all the imperialist cards.

   The main protagonists are now the USA, the USSR,
Israel and the Arab states. The USA and the USSR seek
Arab support. The evolution of the formation and
breaking-up of alliances initially resulted from developments in the Arab liberation movement, and subsequently
from crises within it.

From Nasser to Sadat

A remarkable change took place in the space of twenty
years. In the 1950s and 60s the bulk of the Arab world was
allied to the Soviet Union which provided them with
assistance in many fields. In the ten years after that,

however, there was a general move towards the West.

The Arab liberation movement did not however go through a phase of transition from one side to the other. Initially it achieved a number of undeniable successes. The Arab countries attained real political independence. Not only did they avoid being drawn into the Western-organised regional pacts but they also opposed all foreign military presence in the region. Their foreign policy was a combination of non-alignment and rapprochement with the Soviet Union. Internal transformations got under way: agrarian reform, the establishment of a large public sector, advances in health and education and social progress. Nasser's Egypt is a good example of this.

At the end of the 1960s, after these achievements had been made, other matters came to the fore. The process of emergence from under-development entailed more radical social, political and economic reforms. It also meant breaking off economic dependence on capitalist markets. These revolutionary aspirations went far beyond the abilities of the movement's leaders, whose commitment to independence and the struggle against feudalism did not include major changes and a break with capitalism. They were from petty bourgeois and bourgeois back-grounds, which weakened their resolve, as did the pressure they were under from the new privileged groups created by the reforms, in such areas as agriculture, trade with the West and the government service.

These people were the basis of Sadat's counter-revolution in Egypt and of similar negative phenomena in Iraq and Syria.

Three elements fuelled this degeneration. Firstly the defects of the Arab liberation movement and its lack of democracy. Bourgeois fear of the working class, the poor peasants, and of workers' intervention in general, led them to seize control of the decision-making process and to turn it to the advantage of a small group. This fear, and its consequences, was at a later date to rebound against the nationalists as a whole; they could not mobilise sufficient support to defend what had been won earlier. Thus weakened, and threatened by economic and social difficulties, these regimes became increasingly subject to the influence of the oil-rich kingdoms and emirates in the period after 1973. Saudi Arabia and the Gulf States provided billions of dollars, and their aid had a political pricetag attached to it. And in addition, the exhausting conflict with Israel, the economic and human cost of which was ruinous, led them to seek a compromise that only the United States could pressurise Israel into accepting.

The Arab liberation movement needed new leaders to overcome these obstacles and to set out in new directions. The revolutionary forces had been weakened, particularly the communist parties, who had regularly been the victims of both right and left wing repression. This has hindered the growth of a new leadership, which explains why there has been talk of a 'leadership crisis' within the movement.

Right-wing pro-Americanism is not, however, the whole story in the region. Public opinion and repeated setbacks for President Reagan's policies must not be overlooked, nor should 'the place of the Palestinian question in contemporary Arab political culture'. Ghassan Salame stressed this in an article in *Politique Étrangère* in 1983: 'Whether we like it or not, the Arab-Israeli conflict, because of the West's decisive support for Israel and the terrible plight of the Palestinians, has become a running sore in the conflict with the West which goes back a long way in the history of the Arab world, not to mention the wider Islamic world. Although American experts are able to overlook this fact, the leaders of Saudi Arabia, Kuwait, and even Egypt, live it continually. And even supposing they were able to forget it, there are radio stations in Damascus, Tripoli and even in Tehran, which remind them every day of what happened to Nokrashi Pasha, King Abdullah of Jordan and Anwar Sadat, who were all killed because they forgot this important part of their political culture.'

Pax Americana

This then is the context in which the United States is operating in the Middle East. From the moment when it took charge of imperialist strategy in the region its aims have hardly changed at all: it wants geopolitical control of the area, secure supplies of oil and to seize markets. These objectives depend on the stability of so-called 'moderate' Arab regimes. In order to achieve them the American leaders have adopted four separate approaches in the last forty years.

In the north they have been careful to form close alliances with Turkey – a member of NATO – with Iran, until 1978, and with Pakistan – particularly in the wake of Soviet intervention in Afghanistan. The Cento pact, which was dissolved in 1979, was a series of bilateral treaties to this effect.

But the United States' main ally was and is Israel. The Jewish lobby in America is very strong. The Jewish electorate is considerable: in New York State it amounts to 14% of the registered voters. The way people vote is to a great extent determined by powerful organisations within the Jewish community. Whenever White House statements seem to be at odds with current policy in Tel Aviv, the lobby, both in and out of congress, voices its disagreement. However, although this should not be underestimated, it should be put in perspective. It is a justification, rather than the real reason, for American's quasi-unconditional support for Israel. The basis of America's alliance with Israel is their joint opposition to the Soviet Union and to the Arab liberation movement.

The Israeli leadership's influence in the United States is due to their objective situation: what Israel represents for imperialism is an unparalleled economic and military power in the region with unrivalled political stability. This means that the Israeli leaders have a certain amount of room for manoeuvre in which to pursue their own objectives, and can even oppose their great American ally. The Israelis are well aware of this. Clearly the President of the United States has 'tools' at his disposal that could bring down Tel Aviv in a very short space of time. But who would risk cutting off supplies to such a vitally important ally?

Since the Second World War the White House has tried to win over the Arab states to the struggle against 'Godless communism' whilst maintaining its close ties with Israel. There has been no shortage of initiatives in this direction:

from 'Point IV', to 'Strategic Consensus', as well as the Truman and Eisenhower Doctrines.

In order to back up its claims the United States has long dreamed of having a military force which could use bases and 'facilities' all over the region. They have never ruled out the option of using the Marines. The Middle East has seen them several times: in 1953 in Iran, in 1958 in Beirut, not to mention the American part of the multinational force in Lebanon between August 1982 and March 1984.

These plans have, however, always come up against the immovable obstacle of the Arab-Israeli conflict. The Kuwaiti ambassador to Beirut pointed out in 1979 'that the Soviet threat was becoming old hat. The Kuwaitis had never seen a Soviet invasion of an Arab country but they had seen Israel occupy territory belonging to Arab countries. Similarly they had seen the Israeli occupation of Egypt's oilfields but there had never been a Soviet occupation'. This flawless reasoning brings us back to the endless White House problem of how to square the circle. No one yet has solved it.

Although Kissinger's 'step by step' diplomacy was able to win over Syria and Egypt, it again came up against the Palestinian question. From 1973 the Americans tried to force the issue in two ways. On the one hand they threatened to respond to any danger of revolt in the Arab world by invading to prevent Western oil supplies drying up. In 1980 Jimmy Carter stated that any attempt to control the Gulf would be considered as an attack on American interests and would be resisted in every way possible – including militarily. On the other hand, in order to trap Egypt and Syria into making separate peace agreements, the American tone towards the Palestinians changed: whereas up until 1968 they had just been 'refugees' they became an 'entity' in 1969-70; and they were recognised as having 'legitimate interests' in 1973-74, which became 'rights' in 1975-76 and the right to a 'homeland' in 1977.

Five years later, in 1982, after the invasion of Lebanon, Ronald Reagan thought that he held all the trump cards: a confirmed strategic alliance with Israel, Egypt on the sidelines as a result of the Camp David agreements,

Lebanon controlled by the Phalangists, Syria defeated and the P.L.O. dispersed. The loss of Iranian support was partially made up for by the establishment of the Rapid Deployment Force which, with a maximum strength of 220,000 men, in a string of bases from Morocco to the Indian Ocean, could counter any external intervention as well as internal revolution, particularly in the Gulf. From this secure base the American President set himself two new objectives: to set up a government in Lebanon sympathetic to American interests and to reach some kind of botched up solution to the Palestinian question which would remove the last obstacle in the way of 'strategic consensus'.

As we have shown in the previous chapters it did not take long before bitter disillusion crept in. In the spring of 1984 the balance of power in Lebanon had never been more unfavourable to the Phalangists and their backers. And even the Egyptians and Jordanians have distanced themselves from the Reagan Plan. The US administration needs to redefine its Middle Eastern policy, since the setbacks it has encountered have now given rise to a surge of hostility to interventionism. Without going into the reasons for these setbacks in any detail, one thing is quite clear. The American policymakers have once again underestimated the strength of national groups. Whether Palestinian, Syrian, Lebanese, or Egyptian, the aspirations of the people have shown themselves to be more powerful than the American strategic analysts expected. The same under-estimation is true as far as the Soviet Union is concerned. Here again the Americans were mistaken.

A Reversible Decline

In the immediate post-war period Soviet involvement in the affairs of the Arab world was restricted to Iran and Afganistan, with which it shared frontiers, and to the new-born Israeli state. There was little to encourage further involvement.

It was due to British and American obstinacy that the Soviet Union was able to gain a foothold in the region. Faced with a refusal to supply the arms they demanded to meet the threat posed by Israel, and by an insistence on holding them to the terms of the Baghdad Pact, it was inevitable that the Arab countries would turn to the Soviet Union. Rapprochement with the socialist countries began in September 1955, with an Egyptian order for Czech weapons. At its peak, at the end of the 1960s, Egypt, Syria, Iraq and South Yemen were all receiving aid in some form, whether political, military, economic or cultural.

Yet ten years later almost none of this remains. There are so many reasons for this reversal and they are so complex and intertwined that it is difficult to pinpoint them. Let us try to see the broad outlines. Firstly there was the success of one of the aims of Arab-Soviet solidarity: the end of both civilian and military colonial presence in the Middle East. The second aspect stemmed from the failure of another aim of Arab-Soviet solidarity: that of meeting the aspirations of the Arabs in their conflict with Israel. Other factors relate to the impact of Soviet aid on the countries concerned: whilst in economic and social terms there was remarkable progress, the fundamental problems of development remained. At this juncture it is less a question of the unsuitability of the Soviet model than of the nature of the Arab liberation movements. The initial reforms, and the fact that they were not followed up by more radical changes, had prepared the ground for other political options. Bourgeois and bureaucrats joined forces and turned, doe-eyed, towards the United States, which seemed to be the only country able to both induce Israel to compromise and to meet the Arab countries new 'needs'. Given the lack of clear leadership, class instincts proved more powerful than nationalist consciences. Soviet difficulty in articulating its peaceful coexistence policy left the way clear for such negative tendencies. In the Middle East, as elsewhere, although peaceful coexistence is in the interests of forces engaged in popular struggle, the priority accorded within this strategy to interests of State, and thus to relations between states, can act against revolutionary interests.

The late President Sadat liked to say that the United States had 99% of the cards. This is certainly an exaggeration. Even after Beirut, the Soviet Union, though weakened, is still present. It has three allies: Syria, the P.L.O. and South Yemen. It has not been easy to maintain these alliances, particularly the first two. Damascus, despite repeated disappointments, is still susceptible to the lure of Washington. Hafez Assad attacks the P.L.O. to strengthen his own position. This often makes life difficult for the Soviet Union, since they find themselves torn between two 'friends' who are fighting each other. However these footholds in the region enable the Soviet Union to block any settlement to which it is not a party. Three American presidents ignored this and failed in their efforts in the Middle East. President Reagan's policy has led into a blind alley. It may well be the beginning of an upturn in Soviet fortunes.

The position of the Middle East in Soviet foreign policy is clear: economic factors are only marginal since the Soviet Union spends far more there than it earns, and it is protected by its own oil and gas reserves. On the other hand the region is absolutely vital for its security. Protecting the southern border is an age-old preoccupation of Russian and Soviet policy. It is defensive rather than offensive in character. At the same time the C.P.S.U., following in Lenin's footsteps, and particularly since the 20th Congress, as part of its policy of peaceful coexistence, considers the Arab liberation movement as an important element of the international progressive movement. In Soviet eyes, then, there can be no question of allowing the United States to grab hold of the Middle East. Support for the Arab peoples is, therefore, an important dimension of Soviet strategy.

The Soviet Union is opposed to any partial settlement of the conflict. In Soviet eyes the only way to lay the foundations of peace is by an international conference of all the parties concerned – including the P.L.O. – together with the United States and the USSR. A lasting settlement depends on Israeli withdrawal from the Arab territories occupied since 1967, a guarantee of Israel's right to exist and the creation of a Palestinian state next to it. The Soviet Union is endeavouring to re-establish its influence, and to achieve these ends, by extending the spread of its relations in the Arab world, notably with Jordan, Egypt and Saudi Arabia.

From Cairo to Damascus

The Arab countries are not simply the bones of contention in East-West Super Power rivalry: they have their own reality, evolution and interests. All of them have experienced, though in very different ways, the growth and then the crisis of the liberation movement; yet today they make up a very disparate group of countries indeed. Before ending this book we shall briefly look at the present political situation in each of them.

Egypt occupies a special place in the Arab world. It has the largest population, it is the most powerful economically and militarily and has the most political influence. Egypt has not lost its key role in the Arab world as a result of the Camp David accords. Indeed, since the years of 'treachery' there have been developments in the Egyptian government's position. This change stemmed from the assassination of Sadat and his replacement by Hosni Mubarak in October 1982. The return of Sinai in April 1982 gave the new leader some room for manoeuvre. However this situation ended with the invasion of Lebanon. Egypt withdrew its ambassador from Tel Aviv, called for Israel to withdraw from Lebanon and initiated a rapprochement with the P.L.O. Although the Camp David accords have not been formally abrogated (the autonomy talks however have been indefinitely suspended) and although it has not turned its back on Washington, Egypt has been working to restore its position in the Arab and Islamic world. This has further strengthened its support for a solution to the Palestinian problem that meets with P.L.O. approval. This is exemplified in the meeting between Hosni Mubarak and Yasser Arafat. These foreign policy moves have been accompanied by increased freedom of expression for opposition parties at home. This has led to pressure on the government from disappointed public opinion, feeling let down by the separate peace with Israel, and under the influence of a revitalised left and Islamic activists.

In comparison to the Egyptian giant, Jordan is of little significance. But history has made it the key to Palestine. It was King Abdullah who annexed the West Bank in 1950.

It is still theoretically under Jordanian sovereignty, although it has been occupied by Israel since 1967. At the Arab summit in Fez in 1974 Jordan ceased to have this role when the P.L.O. was declared the sole legitimate representative of the Palestinian people. Whilst accepting this decision King Hussein has not renounced the traditional aims of his regime. Differing currents of opinion advocate contradictory positions. Some favour giving up the West Bank and concentrating on Jordan. Others aim to regain the West Bank and make it an integral part of the Kingdom. They have had a wider audience since the war in Lebanon. It appears that the King is interested in the idea of a Jordano-Palestinian Confederation which would come out of a compromise between Israel, Jordan and Palestinian representatives under American supervision. Hussein is trying to bring this about by pressuring both the Palestinians – by, for example, reactivating the Jordanian Parliament – and the Americans. His insistence on Soviet involvement in the negotiations is an indication of his position. One factor predominates over everything else in Amman: maintaining the stability of the regime in a country in which at least 70% of the population are Palestinian and which Israel insists on calling the Palestinian state. If there were to be another Black September the loser next time might be the ruling dynasty ...

The image of Saudi Arabia and the Gulf States is that of faithful allies of the United States. True, they are fiercely anti-communist and pro-western. They have shown this time and time again, most significantly by continuing to supply the west with oil, except during the brief 1973 embargo. One essential element divides them from the United States: the Palestinians. In their eyes the main reason for instability in the region is the lack of a Palestinian state. This in turn stimulates popular movements and allows the Soviet Union into Middle Eastern affairs. Ryadh's pretensions to the leadership of the Arab and Islamic world will never materialise without the liberation of the Holy Places in Jerusalem, and the creation of a Palestinian State. These aims are born out by Fatah's long-established relations with the Saudi leadership as well as by the demographic and economic importance of the Palestinian community in the

Gulf. Or at least there is a strong verbal commitment: Saudi Arabia and the Gulf States have always been careful not to 'arm' themselves in any real sense, in order to obtain substantial concessions from the United States.

Iraq is very much on the margins of the Arab world. Its contribution to the struggle against Israel has never consisted of anything more than sending a few symbolic battalions to the frontline. But this has not prevented it from being the most hardline state of all: indeed it harboured and nurtured the dissident Palestinian group led by Abu Nidal for many years. Iraq's position has become more realistic in recent years, following a rapprochement with more moderate Arab states; but the bloody war with Iran rules out any involvement in activity in the Middle East.

1983 has quite rightly been called the year of Syria. Egypt's removal from the scene following the Camp David accords, and Iraq's involvement in war elsewhere, thrust Syria into the spotlight. Those who are fond of plumbing the Baathist soul usually claim to find traces of nostalgia for the Ummayad Empire and 'Greater Syria'. Part of Hafez Assad's policies they may be, but not a central one. Above all else Syria fears being surrounded: a Phalangist Lebanon under Israeli-American control would complete a ring which already comprises two hostile neighbours in Jordan and Iraq. Popular aspirations focus on the liberation of the Golan Heights which Israel occupied in 1967 and annexed in 1981. Syria also has obvious ambitions on a regional level as well as these defensive considerations. Since coming to terms with its defeat in 1982, the Damascus regime has been endeavouring, with some success, to retrieve its position: the military has been strengthened thanks to a tenfold increase in Soviet aid; it has a massive presence in Lebanon in close alliance with the opposition there, and it has tried, to date without success, to control the P.L.O. Some people express surprise at the contradictions of a strategy which on the one hand turns down American plans, and on the other launches an all-out assault against Yasser Arafat. Syria appears to be an anti-imperialist stronghold, and yet at the same time is ready to discuss new plans to carve out areas of influence in the region with the United States. The background to this ambiguity is Syrian society, which is in the grip of the internal developments mentioned above, from which the entire Arab nationalist movement has suffered.

De Gaulle

Finally, there is one other country that counts in the Middle East: France. Although it was the first country to have dealings with the Ottoman empire, it was gradually pushed out of the area from the beginning of the nineteenth century by British hegemony, in circumstances which we described in the first chapter. After the Suez fiasco and the Algerian war, France had no role left at all, except in Israel, which the Fourth Republic governments, and socialist leaders in particular, viewed with warm approval. It was not until de Gaulle's courageous attitude during and after the Six Day War that France began to emerge from this eclipse. De Gaulle was shocked by the Tel Aviv government's aggression, and condemned both the occupation of the Arab territories and the annexation of Jerusalem. He responded to Israeli intransigence by a strict arms embargo to all the 'Confrontation States', starting with the Israeli state. Ever since then his name has been part of the collective memory of the Arabs.

This change of policy marked the start of a renewal of French influence in the Arab world. De Gaulle's successors – Georges Pompidou as well as Valéry Giscard d'Estaing – followed in his footsteps. In effect they are implementing the approach favoured by the French Communist Party. The Élysée and the Quai d'Orsay have sided with the Arab peoples and backed their demands for a just peace settlement. The French Foreign Office was one of the first in Europe to have relations with the P.L.O., who were allowed to open an office in Paris in 1975. France is an advocate of 'Palestinian National Rights' within the E.E.C. During the same period the old policy of 'protecting' Lebanon has recurred. Of course there are also economic aspects of this policy: French capital has seized the

opportunity presented by this new friendship to gain a
foothold in Middle Eastern markets. In the years since
1970 important agreements have been signed with Iraq,
Egypt, Saudi Arabia, Libya, Iran and others. In return for
oil France sells arms, high technology and, most important
of all, nuclear power stations, not forgetting countless
consumer goods.

The Left's victory in the 1981 French elections gave rise
to considerable concern about what the foreign policy of
the new government might be, given the traditional
friendship between the Socialist Party and Israel.
Although these fears were allayed for a time by President
Mitterrand's support for the Fahad Plan and by Foreign
Minister Cheysson's declarations on the creation of a
Palestinian state, and his meeting with Arafat, they were
underlined by Mitterrand's state visit to Israel in March
1982. But Menachem Begin's insult to Mitterrand during
the visit, followed by the invasion of Lebanon, prompted
the French government to adopt a clearer stance. It had a
key role first in saving the P.L.O in Beirut and then
evacuating them from Tripoli. There are still ambiguities
and contradictions, but overall the left-wing government
has seen De Gaulle's Middle Eastern policy bear fruit.

In setting itself up to defend the rights of the people by
striving to obtain a fair and lasting settlement our country
has regained some of the prestige which the French
people's revolutionary and democratic traditions had
earned in the Arab world. Peace between Israel and its
neighbours, respecting the rights of all the peoples
concerned, is a matter of concern both for our
government and for all of us.

The Future

Now that we are at the end of this study it is clear that
there is not just one conflict in the Middle East; there are
many. First of all there is the conflict between Israel and
the Palestinians, which has led to one between Israel and
the Arab world. The religious and political divisions which
have always existed in Lebanon have become intolerable.
Added to this are the traditional rivalries between the

Arab countries, and their resistance to any hegemonic influence in the region. Lastly there is the great powers' involvement in the conflict and what is at stake for them – the old 'Eastern Question' all over again. The West seeks to safeguard its domination at all costs while the Soviet Union, though supporting the liberation movements, is mindful of its own interests. American imperialism is kept at bay here, as it has been for a long time.

There is no miraculous way out of the impasse. Each and every local and regional conflict needs to be resolved individually. Stability will not be achieved without the participation and agreement of all the interested parties. Without this no agreement, and certainly no global agreement, has any chance of success. This is particularly true of the conflict between Jews and Arabs for control of Palestine, which is at the heart of this Hundred Years War. A peaceful outcome to this conflict is necessary for a more general peace, although not sufficient in itself. Coexistence between the two peoples who claim the 'Holy Land' as theirs would surely bring about an early peace throughout the whole of the Middle East.

By way of conclusion it is then fitting that we should briefly look at the different solutions that have been put forward, examine their advantages and disadvantages and the chances of their being implemented. Here there are six basic options.

Let us start with the two extremes. The dream of annexing the occupied territories – the West Bank of the Jordan and South Lebanon – is still part of the programme of the Herut Party and an underlying, if not openly avowed, aim of the Tel Aviv government. Israeli aspirations to control all of Palestine stem from an unjust and unreal conception which ignores the reality of the Palestinian nation whose unwillingness to disappear has been proven in decades of struggle. Their resistance, and the regional and international power relations, show the illusory nature of any such radical denial of their rights. Such a thing would not be permitted. Moreover pacifists in Israel have pointed out that if Israel were to absorb another million Arabs it would be difficult to preserve the democratic Jewish state: it would either have to safeguard its Judaic nature by abandoning democracy or lose it by remaining democratic. So the annexationist demands made by the theocratic fascists of the Gush Emunim group have to be firmly rejected on grounds of justice and common sense.

The same is true of the liberation of Palestine, as defined by the borders it had during the British mandate; this definition appears in the 1968 P.L.O. National Charter which the Fatah dissidents have been brandishing. In any case the Palestinian National Council have *de facto* abandoned this objective since their 1974 demand for the creation of a Palestinian state 'On every part of Palestinian land to be liberated'. As we have seen this evolution has been confirmed and extended on many occasions. Rightly so: the destruction of the state of Israel would be as unrealistic and unjust an aim as the first option we examined. A nation has been moulded together by the *Yishuv*, and the State of Israel, which has as much right as any other to peace and security, despite the expansionism of its leaders. In any case the regional and worldwide context would rule out such a utopian perspective for the foreseeable future. No-one can disagree that it would be a nice idea if there were a state of Palestine in which Jews, Muslims and Christians would all live together freely as equals. The people and their governments could decide to do so but clearly it will not come about for at least a few centuries.

The American plan can be summed up by the word 'autonomy'. That was the second phase of the Camp David accords which have never been implemented. President Reagan resurrected it in his speech on 1 September 1982. In passing we should note that the Israeli government, which had accepted the first version of 'autonomy', vehemently rejected the second. The president, recognising that the Palestinian problem is a national problem, not a question of refugees, saw a two-stage solution. During the first stage, which would take five years, the people of Gaza and the West Bank would have 'absolute autonomy in managing their own affairs': they – including the people in East Jerusalem – would elect their own administration to which power would be transferred. The second stage would consist of defining their status as 'associated with Jordan'.

The various 'Jordanian options' suggested in Israel and elsewhere have one thing in common with the 'autonomy' favoured by the United States: none of them accept the principle of self determination for the Palestinians. General Sharon saw this as 'giving' Jordan – which he sees as the only Palestinian state – to the P.L.O., in return for the P.L.O.'s abandoning claims to the West Bank and Gaza. Shimon Peres and the Labour Party on the other hand want to negotiate a 'territorial compromise' with King Hussein: Jordan would regain part of the West Bank, with Israel retaining large agricultural, residential or military settlements. In the words of the secretary of the Israeli Human Rights League, Joseph Algazy it would be a 'Hashemite-ruled Palestinian sausage in an Israeli sandwich' and would, like the Sharon proposal, deny the Palestinians the right to set up their own state and in the meantime to be represented by the P.L.O. The situation becomes even more complex when the status of Jerusalem is taken into consideration. Israel annexed the Arab part and declared Jerusalem the capital of the Israeli state. The Fez plan, adopted by the P.L.O., sees it as the capital of the Palestinian state. For President Reagan it will just remain 'undivided'; everything else is a matter for negotiation. The past and the present have produced two requirements which are difficult to reconcile. Jerusalem is a Holy City for three of the most important world religions. It would not suit religious people for it to be split and for access to the Holy Places to be made difficult. The undivided city is a denial of the aspirations of the two peoples who claim Jerusalem as their capital. A new formula will certainly need to be devised at some stage. Meanwhile both Israel and a future Palestinian state can demand equal rights, which should be part of a transitional agreement.

One thing comes out of this schematic review very clearly: today, the only solution which is morally and politically acceptable is for there to be two states, one Israeli and one Palestinian, coexisting side by side. Indeed this was the core of the Arab plan agreed at Fez. This is fundamental. But so too is a second, equally important factor: the creation of such a Palestinian state will be blocked for the foreseeable future for reasons relating to regional and international considerations. Israel rejects such a solution out of hand and, although weaker than it was, it still has the power to do so. The United States reject it, and their voice does not go unheard in the Middle East. And the Arab states themselves would not look favourably on this dangerous precedent if ever it were to materialise.

What will history do, faced with the choice between justice and injustice, the desirable and the possible, the real and the unreal? Anyone who tries to answer such questions about the Middle East is extremely foolish. People who guess never get it right. So complex are the problems, so quickly do times change, so frequent are the turns of events, that the best guesses are proved wrong. The Middle East conflict has many aspects. Despite setbacks and crises over the years, the Palestinian Resistance has learnt to come to terms with them and to put forward realistic peace proposals. After lengthy discussion it initially declared its support for 'the independent authority of the people in struggle over every liberated part of the territory of Palestine'. Then, during the siege of Beirut, came the famous handwritten document signed by Yasser Arafat which accepted 'the United Nations resolutions as a whole'. This has since been reaffirmed several times, although Resolution 242 on its own has been rejected. Finally, the Arab plan drawn up at Fez, and the Brezhnev Plan, which both call for coexistence between Israel and a Palestinian state on the West Bank and in Gaza, have been approved by the Palestine National Council at meetings in Algiers and Amman.

Recognition of the gap between what is desirable and what is possible has recently led the P.L.O. some way down the road towards the 'Jordano-Palestinian' formula which it previously rejected. The idea of 'confederation with Jordan' was approved by the Palestine National Council meeting in Algiers in 1983 and reaffirmed at the Amman meeting the following year. But we must distinguish this from the American, Israeli and Jordanian dream of 'confederation'. For the Palestinian Resistance it implies that a Palestinian state would rule the present occupied territories, that exiled Palestinians would be allowed to return or be indemnified, and that the P.L.O. would negotiate all this. It is easy to see that this has nothing in common with the ideas of Reagan or Peres or even of some of the Jordanian leaders.

The Jordano-Palestinian agreement of February 1985 shows that Arafat and the P.L.O. Executive Committee, the latter somewhat reluctantly, are prepared to make even more concessions, and risk worsening the crisis in the movement. While reaffirming the conditions and principles of a just and lasting settlement the text defines its aim as 'the formation of a confederation of the Arab states of Jordan and Palestine'. It states that this should be achieved by international negotiation, in which 'the P.L.O., sole legitimate representative of the Palestinian people, should be part of a joint Jordano-Palestinian delegation'. This position is theoretically in accordance with the line adopted at the 16th and 17th Palestine National Councils, provided that the negotiations meet two conditions which, for the Palestinians, are vitally important: first, and prior to any negotiation, the acceptance of an independent Palestinian state in federation with Jordan and the presence of truly representative Palestinian representatives in the planned joint delegation. In addition to this is the issue of the nature of the negotiations: whether it should be an international conference with great power participation, including the Soviet Union; or a separate agreement solely under the aegis of the United States? Israel's position remains intransigent, as usual, but the White House seemed to be becoming more flexible. Just how flexible remains to be seen.

The outcome depends on a number of factors. Will opposition to the economic crisis and the anti-war movement in Israel become strong enough to force the government to accept a viable peace agreement? Will United States interests best be served by a peace agreement that ensures their continuing influence in an area where the Palestinian problem is a constant threat to positions held by the United States and its Arab allies? What happens will also depend on developments in the Arab world: on what Egypt may contribute as it seeks to regain its leadership role; on Syrian readiness to make compromises to protect its key role; on concern in Saudi Arabia and the Gulf States about the destabilising effect of the conflict: on Jordanian fears of possible reper- cussions amongst its population, the majority of whom are Palestinian; and, not least, on the Iran-Iraq war which is draining the energy of both sides. There is also the question of international influence – or the lack of it – primarily from Europe. Perhaps France could help to revitalise the impact made by the famous Venice Declaration. Finally it depends on the P.L.O. itself and whether or not it is able to reunite the Palestinian movement in a credible, independent offensive position.

History will decide. A few years ago there was a slogan painted on a wall in Beirut by the D.F.L.P. which read 'We shall never be the Indians of the Middle East'. Since the Israeli invasion of Lebanon this is very much the core of what has been at stake. All popular causes are just, but not all of them win. The Palestinians deserve to win. Their history, struggle, culture and intelligence have made them a great people whose voice cannot be forgotten in regional and international affairs. Their numbers, their conscious- ness and their determination have made them indispen- sable to peace in the Middle East and in the world. So many opportunities have been lost in the past century. Isn't it time to seize one?

Brief Chronology 1896-1986

1896: Publication of Theodore Herzl's *The Jewish State*.
August: World Zionist Movement founded at the Basle Congress.
1908: Young Turk Revolution.
1914 October: Ottoman Empire enters the First World War on the side of the Central Powers.
1916 May: Secret Sykes-Picot Agreement between Britain, France and Russia to divide the Middle East.
June: Start of the Arab revolt.
1917 November: Balfour Declaration.
1920 May: The Allies divide the Ottoman Empire at the San Remo Conference.
1922 July: The League of Nations places Palestine under British Mandate.
1933 January: Hitler achieves power. Growth of Jewish emigration to Palestine.
1936-39: Palestinian Revolt.
1937: Peel Commission proposes the partition of Palestine.
1939 May: British Government White Paper aims to halt Jewish immigration.
1947 February: after increasing confrontations in Palestine the British Government decides to refer the matter to the U.N.
1947 November: UN General Assembly adopts the Palestine partition plan by a two thirds majority.
1948 April: Irgun terrorists massacre in Palestinian village of Deir Yassin.
1948 May: Proclamation of the state of Israel. The Arab states reject the partition plan and invade on 15 May.
1948-49: War ends in victory for Israel. Armistices signed

between Israel and its Arab neighbours.

1950 April: Jordan annexes the West Bank. Egypt annexes Gaza shortly afterwards.

1952: Free Officers overthrow the monarchy in Egypt. Nasser becomes unchallenged leader two years later.

1955 February: Baghdad Pact signed. 28 February: Israel attacks Gaza.

1956 July: Nationalisation of the Suez canal. October-November: Israel, France and Britain attack Egypt.

1958 February: Union of Egypt and Syria in the United Arab Republic.

May: American intervention in Jordan and in the Lebanese Civil War.

July: Fall of the monarchy in Iraq.

1961 September: Split of Egypt and Syria.

1962 September: Revolution in Yemen.

1964 January: First Arab summit conference in Cairo.

1964 May: Creation of the P.L.O.

1965 January: Fatah launches its first attack against Israel.

1967 June: Israel attacks Egypt and Syria. At the end of the Six Day War in Sinai, the Golan Heights, the West Bank and Gaza are occupied. June: U.N. Security Council resolution 242.

1968 March: Battle between Israeli and Palestinian troops at Karameh.

July: 4th Palestine National Council adopts National Charter.

1969 January-February: 5th Palestine National Council. Yasser Arafat becomes president of the Executive Committee.

November: Cairo accords between Lebanon and the P.L.O. after a number of incidents in Lebanon.

1970 February: serious conflicts between the P.L.O. and the Jordanian government.

July: Nasser and Hussein accept the Rogers plan to implement Resolution 242.

September: 'Black September': fighting between the P.L.O. and the Jordanian Army.

September: death of Nasser.

1970-71 P.L.O. expelled from Jordan. Headquarters set up in Lebanon.

1973 April: Israeli operation in Beirut. Three important P.L.O. leaders assassinated. Large demonstrations of solidarity with the P.L.O. in Lebanon.

August: Palestinian National Front set up in the occupied territories.

October: Egypt and Syria attacked Israel. Start of the October War, also known as the Yom Kippur war.

October: Security Council Resolution 338. Conflict ceases a few days later.

November: Arab summit in Algiers. P.L.O. recognised as the sole legitimate representative of the Palestinian people. Jordan abstains on this issue.

1974 June: 12th Palestine National Council. P.L.O. accepts the idea of authority over all liberated territories. The rejectionist front is created a few weeks later.

October: Arab summit in Rabat. Jordan accepts the majority view and recognises the P.L.O.

November: Yasser Arafat speech at the UN. UN recognition of the Palestinians' right to self determination and a homeland. Observer status granted to P.L.O.

1975 April: start of civil war in Lebanon.

1976 January: first Syrian intervention in Lebanon.

April: local elections on the West Bank. Victory for P.L.O. sympathisers.

June: massive Syrian military intervention in Lebanon against the P.L.O. and the Lebanese National Movement.

August: Tall el Zaatar Palestinian refugee camp surrenders after 57 days siege.

September: the P.L.O. is admitted to the Arab league as a full member.

1977 March: 13th Palestine National Council. Acceptance of a Palestinian state on part of the territory of Palestine.

May: first P.L.O.–Communist Party of Israel meeting in Prague.

May: Begin wins elections in Israel and becomes Prime Minister.

October: joint Soviet-American declaration on peace in the Middle East, supported by the P.L.O.

November: Sadat visits Jerusalem.

December: Hard line front set up in Tripoli comprising

Libya, Algeria, Syria, South Yemen and the P.L.O.
1978 March: Israel invades South Lebanon.
September: Camp David accords between USA, Egypt and Israel.
November: End of Arab summit in Baghdad condemns Camp David accords.
1979 February: Ayatollah Khomeini returns to Tehran.
March: Peace Treaty between Israel and Egypt signed in Washington.
July: Arafat, Kreisky and Brandt meeting in Vienna.
1980 2 June: Mayors of Nablus and Ramallah seriously injured in bomb attacks.
July: Knesset votes a law proclaiming 'reunified' Jerusalem the capital of Israel.
September: start of Iran–Iraq war.
1981 July: War between Israel and Palestine on the Lebanese border. Israeli bombings of Beirut. Israeli attack on Osirak nuclear reactor at Tamuz.
August: Peace plan proposed by Crown Prince Fahd of Saudi Arabia.
October: Sadat assassinated.
November: Failure of Arab summit in Fez.
December: Israel annexes Golan.
1982 March-April: Palestinian uprisings in occupied territories. Elected mayors sacked.
April: Israel completes evacuation of Sinai.
June: start of Israeli invasion of Lebanon. Siege of Beirut begins a few days later.
August: P.L.O. evacuation of Beirut under supervision of international peacekeeping force.
September: President Reagan's peace plan.
September: Final resolution of Fez Arab Summit.
September: Bashir Gemayel assassinated. Israelis enter West Beirut. Sabra and Chatila massacres.
September: Brezhnev peace plan.
September: Amin Gemayel elected president of Lebanon.
1983 January: Arafat, Avnery, Peled meeting in Paris.
February: 16th Palestine National Council meeting in Algiers.
April: Failure of Arafat-Hussein negotiations.
April: Assassination of Issam Sartawi at International

Socialist Congress in Portugal.

May: start of dissidence within Fatah.

May: Israel – Lebanon peace agreement.

August-September: renewal of civil war in Lebanon. Druze take control of the Shouf. Begin resigns, replaced by Shamir.

October: Start of Geneva conference on Lebanon.

November: start of siege of Tripoli by Syria and dissident Palestinians.

November: exchange of six Israeli soldiers for almost 1500 Palestinian prisoners.

December: 4000 Arafat loyalists leave Tripoli aboard Greek ships under French protection.

December: Arafat – Mubarak meeting.

1984 February: Amin Gemayel debacle. Wazzan government resigns. Shiite Amal militia take control of West Beirut. Walid Jumblat's Progressive Socialist Party control the mountains. US marines, British and Italian troops leave Beirut.

March: abrogation of 17 May 1983 Lebanon-Israel accords by Amin Gemayel.

March: failure of Lausanne conference.

March: fall of Shamir government following vote of censure.

April: French soldiers leave Beirut, accompanied by Foreign Minister Cheysson and Defence Minister Hernu.

April: Rashid Karameh appointed head of National Unity Government in Lebanon.

June-July: Negotiations between Fatah and the Democratic Alliance result in Aden-Algiers accord. However it is not implemented.

July: Elections in Israel. Establishment of National Unity government led by Shimon Peres.

October-November: Re-establishment of relations between Egypt and Jordan.

November: 17th Palestine National Council in Amman in the absence of the Democratic Alliance and the pro-Syrians.

1985 January: in the light of deadlocked negotiations with the Lebanese government and increasing armed resistance Israel begins to withdraw from South Lebanon in three stages.

February: Arafat-Hussein agreement on joint diplomatic action.

February: Israeli army evacuates Sidon.

March: National Salvation Front set up in Damascus bringing together the pro-Syrian Palestinian organisations and the P.F.L.P. This is criticised by the D.F.L.P. and the P.C.P.

March-April: violent confrontations in the Sidon area provoked by the Lebanese armed forces. Religious massacres lead to a Christian exodus towards Jezzine, South Lebanon and the Beirut area. End of phase two of the Israeli withdrawal.

May: start of the Amal-Lebanese army offensive against the Palestinian refugee camps in Beirut.

May: Hussein visit to Washington.

June: End of Israeli withdrawal from Lebanon, except for border strip controlled by South Lebanese Army under pro-Israeli General Lahad.

October: Israeli air force raid on P.L.O. headquarters in Tunis. 70 dead.

October: Italian ship *Achille Lauro* hijacked.

October: Shimon Peres at the UN offers Jordan direct negotiation under an international umbrella if necessary.

November: Hijacking of Air Egypt Boeing to Malta.

December: terrorist attacks at Rome and Vienna airports.

1986 January: Interchristian fighting leads to departure of Elie Hobeika.

February: Jordano-Palestinian negotiations fail to secure P.L.O. acceptance of 242 without American guarantees of P.L.O. participation in any future international conference. Hussein abrogates the Jordano-Palestinian accord.

March: assassination of Israeli-imposed mayor of Nablus.

11-12 September: first Mubarak-Peres meeting in Alexandria.

October: Shamir becomes Prime Minister of Israel.

Index